MYTHS and [illegible]
PUZZLES and [illegible]ICS

TALES FROM FOUR SHIRES:

Buckinghamshire, Bedfordshire, Hertfordshire & Northamptonshire

by
John Houghton

All Royalties to

OXFAM

By the same author in this series:

Murders and Mysteries, People and Plots.
Eccentrics and Villains, Hauntings and Heroes.

First published May 1995
by
The Book Castle
12 Church Street
Dunstable
Bedfordshire LU5 4RU

ISBN 1 871199 82 4

Front cover: 'Peasants Paying Tithes' by a follower of Pieter Brueghel.

Computer typeset by Keyword, Aldbury, Hertfordshire.
Printed by Antony Rowe Ltd., Chippenham.

CONTENTS

LIST OF ILLUSTRATIONS

PREFACE

Edmund Burke wrote: 'People will not look forward to posterity who never look back to their ancestors'.

Looking back to our ancestors in our four mid-Anglia shires of Bucks., Beds., Herts., and Northants. reveals much that is astonishing, and plenty to shock us.

Personalities abound, some amusing, some heroic, and some discreditable!

Some myths are exploded by reality, and some facts cause us wonder and surprise.

'Social History is the story of the long march of Everyman.' So, as Everyman marches towards posterity he learns much from looking back to the past.

John Houghton

Also by John Houghton:

Borrowed Time Extended
Tales from Milton Keynes
Murders & Mysteries, People & Plots
Eccentrics & Villains, Hauntings & Heroes

ABOUT THE AUTHOR

John Houghton was born in Eastbourne in 1916. After graduating at Durham University he was ordained in 1939. After a Curacy at Wolverton (1939–42) he served in Northern Rhodesia/Zambia 1942–73. He received the Zambian Order of Distinguished Service in 1966 and is a Canon Emeritus of Lusaka Cathedral. He retired in 1983 and lived in Bletchley.

BIBLIOGRAPHY

E.S.Roscoe: Buckinghamshire
R.L.Greenall: A History of Northamptonshire
C.Hibbert: The English – A Social History
Asa Briggs: A Social History of England
Brewer: Dictionary of Phrase and Fable
John Hassell: A Tour of the Grand Junction Canal in 1819
Ivor Guest: Dr John Radcliffe and His Trust
Buckinghamshire Sessions Records, Volume I

Chapter 1

'Curiouser and Curiouser', Cried Alice

About 120 years ago Robert Gibbs of Aylesbury published a series of volumes in which he collected together, in chronological order, hundred of news items and historical references over the centuries, from the middle ages up to his own times. Thus he saved for posterity any number of odd and quirky items, including many concerning our region. Here is a selection of them.

Old Church Registers, likewise, sometimes yield fascinating items which are intriguing or odd. So a few of them, from Thornton Church Registers, are included here too.

1561 November 19th. 'The manufacture of needles has been resumed at Long Crendon by a person of the name of Christopher Greening. His children assist him, and the numbers they make is astonishing'.

❖❖❖❖❖

1630 October 30th. 'Watches were such a rarity at this period that it is said a Dr Allen, who had the reputation of being a wizard, happening to leave his watch in a bedroom in a house where he was visiting in the country, came near to losing it because a chambermaid who found it thought it was the doctor's "familiar spirit". She therefore took it up with a pair of tongs and threw it out of the window into the moat "to drown the devil". But, "as one who is born to be hanged cannot be drowned", the watch, when search was made for it, was found hanging in a bush growing in the bank of the moat, on which it had accidentally caught in its flight through the air. This failure in her attempt only the more confirmed the girl in her idea, and she could not be prevailed upon to touch the watch again'.

❖ ❖ ❖ ❖ ❖

1661 August 18th. 'Collected for Henry Harrison, Mariner, who had suffered 7500 li by shipwracke, ye summe of three shillings and two pence'.

1663. 'Collected for Dundulo ye Turke three shillings.

(Thornton Register)

❖ ❖ ❖ ❖ ❖

1686 July 11th. 'Elizabeth Pater, widow, was buried after having lyen about seven weeks without any evacuation downwards and most of ye time not upwards neither'.

❖ ❖ ❖ ❖ ❖

1687. 'Francis Harvise was buried in Woollen. He died of a cancer in his eye wch had several years (5 or 6 or more) afflicted him and eaten into his head'.

(Woollen is not the village where he died. The Register is simply recording the fact that he was buried in a woollen shroud, as required by an Act passed in 1667. The purpose of the Act was to encourage and promote the wool trade.)

❖ ❖ ❖ ❖ ❖

1689. 'Richard ye sone of William How and Elizabeth his wife was baptised 15th day of September. (Called out of Church in midst of sermon to baptise it, bee likely to die.)

❖ ❖ ❖ ❖ ❖

1695. 'Francis Colman dyed March 3rd, but was not buried in this parish because he died excommunicate, and was fecht by some Anabapt brethren to a Burying place of theirs at Stony Stratford'.

❖ ❖ ❖ ❖ ❖

1716 January 14th. 'The Thames is now become one solid block of ice; coaches, carriers with their horses and their wagons have passed like a public road; booths for the sale of brandy, wine and ale, and other liquors, have been fixed there for some time. But now it is made in manner like a town; thousands of people cross it, and with wonder view the mountainous heaps of water than now lie congealed into ice, notwithstanding the resistance given to the cold by the movement of the tide. A pretty large cook's shop was erected on the ice. Over against Westminster Hall, Whitehall, and White Friars printing presses are kept upon the ice, where thousands of people have their names printed off, to transmit the wonders of the season to their children'.

❖❖❖❖❖

1841 July 29th. 'The Dissenters at Fenny Stratford are divided into two sections, the result of a quarrel. They are distinguished by the very classic appellations of the potato party and the cauliflower party'.

❖❖❖❖❖

1842. 'There is a person at Owlswick who is uncle to himself, brother to his father, and granduncle to his own children. These children have a grandmother who is their aunt, and a grandfather who is their uncle; and uncles and aunts who are their first cousins'.

❖❖❖❖❖

1844 October 12th. 'This week a gentleman went courting at Quainton on horseback; he was so absorbed in the object of his visit that he forgot his horse and walked three miles home'.

❖❖❖❖❖

1845 February 22nd. 'An old woman died last week aged 109. Her name was Betty Heath. When 50 years old she was thought to be dead, and was about to be screwed down, when she kicked up her heels, and took another lease for 59 years'.

❖❖❖❖❖

1849 August 4th. 'The Aylesbury Luggage engine made off alone last night before the time of starting. It dashed through the gates at the crossing and smashed them. Pursuit was made, but the engine had the best of it, and continued its course until it reached Leighton Station where it gave up, being exhausted for want of fuel'.

❖❖❖❖❖

1871 September 2nd. 'A remarkable cure of a woman of the name of Webb, a pauper in the Wycombe Union, has been made. She had been bed-ridden 23 years at her own home, and chargeable all that time. Further outdoor relief was refused and she was removed to the House. Not liking her new home, she got up and walked four miles back to her home at Prestwood. So the cure was complete'.

❖❖❖❖❖

1879 April 8th. 'For 210 years a ceremony has been observed at Worminghall on Good Friday when 33 new shillings and 66 loaves are distributed at Church to parishioners. Each recipient drops 1d into the hat of the Parish Clerk, for which he cleans a brass tablet in the church belonging to the family of King, members of which were bishops of London and Chichester'.

❖❖❖❖❖

1880 August 1st. 'A poor fellow at Woburn who has lost three wives, has had them photographed in a group, including his own likeness. Looking forward to number four, he had added this touching inscription: "The Lord will provide".'

❖❖❖❖❖

Sir Jeremy Sandbrook owned an estate at North Mimms in Hertfordshire. Early in the 18th century he built a great arch, flanked with two towers suitably castellated. An avenue of trees led away from the arch but, oddly, the avenue led nowhere. Some say Sir Jeremy built the arch as a memorial to commemorate the Battle of Barnet. (See Chapter 16) but it bears no inscription to the effect. Another rumour about the arch says that the builder placed a farthing coin under every single brick. Some 20,000 bricks were needed for the arch. While it is true that 20,000 farthings would only amount to £20, we would have to multiply that sum many times over to convert the 18th century money into today's value. But in any case, why put farthings into the brickwork? Curiouser and curiouser.

❖❖❖❖❖

In the 1830s George Proctor of Benington in Hertfordshire built a Folly. He already owned a late 17th century house. He set to work to add to it in a bewildering range of architectural styles. Some of the additions were deliberately built as ruins. He added a gateway with castellated towers and a portcullis; a number of other gateways were also added, deliberately leading nowhere. Then a courtyard was constructed surrounded by intentionally-ruined walls. There was also a moat and a ruined tower, and finally, a shrine to Buddha!

❖❖❖❖❖

Wealthy landowners have often spent their money to build follies. Usually the motive is to add interest to the view to be enjoyed from their houses, by erecting on distant hilltops a tower, a sham castle, or an obelisk. But there are examples of follies being built right at, or even on top of the owner's house. The retired Admiral Straten, of Little Berkhamsted in Hertfordshire provides an example.

At his house he built an observatory. It is well designed and well built. Yet it entirely failed to provide the Admiral with what he wanted. He hadn't built the observatory to observe the heavens. He built it so that from it he could cure his nostalgia by sitting on top of it with his telescope to observe the ships on the Thames. It proved a geographical miscalculation – it was impossible to see any such ships from Hertfordshire. It is to be hoped that in his sea-going days his navigation was less faulty!

❖❖❖❖❖

Whoever designed the Vicarage at Harrington in Northamptonshire evidently thought it would be appropriate to give a genuine ecclesiastical flavour to its roof. So not content with providing the house with a conventional chimney, he designed one that would look exactly like a church steeple. It is constructed in such a way that the smoke does not emerge at the top; it escapes through holes hidden in the sides of the 'steeple'.

❖❖❖❖❖

The river Ouse runs through Turvey in Bedfordshire. In mid-stream there is a statue. It is in the form of a fisherman holding a fish. The statue is of uncertain origin. It was found in the river. Some thought it was a representation of St. Peter and wondered if it had once stood in a church. But how did it come to be in the river? When it was found there, a Coroner's Court sat to try to determine its ownership. This proved impossible, so the Coroner's verdict was that it should be returned to the river, but properly erected, to stand there in mid-stream.

❖❖❖❖❖

A discovery of a different sort occasioned this item:
1713 October 4th. 'John, reputed son of Catherine Cartwright, of Leckhamstead (found hanging in a basket on the gates which open out of the great yard into the Highway) was baptised 4 October 1713'.

Chapter 2

North Bucks Rules, OK ?

Separated by about 180 years, there are two periods in British history when North Bucks exercised phenomenal influence on national affairs. Though totally different from each other, the reality of the influence each exerted cannot be denied. In both cases contemporary society was unaware of what was happening at two places in North Bucks. The two places, within a dozen miles of each other, were Stowe and Bletchley.

The Powerhouse of Stowe

It was Sir Frank Markham who used that phrase to describe the remarkable influence and importance of Stowe. To justify it, he quoted a speech made by the Earl of Rosebery in 1804 at Aylesbury. The Earl was a former Prime Minister, and in that speech he said:

'Politics have been the pride of Bucks. Her political position was achieved in the 18th century and lasted until politics passed out of the hands of the grandees and became popular and democratic. I claim for Bucks that she is the most famous of English counties in the field of politics during that period.'

'Why was this? The reason seems to lie in the Palace of Stowe and its inhabitants. The political power began under the fostering influence of Lord Cobham, and at Stowe there was gathered that remarkable group known as the Cobham Cousins – Grenvilles, Lyttletons and Pitts. The political power of Stowe continued through long generations.'

Within the space of forty years the Stowe group provided no less than four Prime Ministers: George Grenville, 1763–65;

William Pitt, 1766–67; William Pitt 'The Younger', 1783–1801 and 1804–06; and William Grenville, 1806–07.

The explanation is that all of them were members of that Stowe Group. Stowe became the hub of British politics, truly a power in the land. It was the dynamo which powered so much of what was planned and done.

How did all this come about? Stowe was the seat of Sir Richard Temple (1669–1749). He was the local MP and had been made a Baron in 1714. In 1718 he was raised to the peerage as Lord Cobham. He died without children and Stowe passed to his sister, Hester Temple, a remarkable woman.

Hester married Richard Grenville of Wotten Underwood, the owner of several manors in Mid-Bucks. After Richard Grenville died Hester was made Countess Temple. She became a great political hostess and the tradition for great political meetings at Stowe began.

Of Hester's children, Richard, Earl Temple was both an MP and Cabinet Minister; her second son, George, became Prime Minister in 1763; her daughter, also called Hester, married in 1754 a young politician named William Pitt, (later Earl of Chatham) who in 1766 became Prime Minister.

So Stowe became a great political centre and powerhouse. Of the next generation, the second son of Hester and William Pitt (always known as Pitt the Younger) went on to become Prime Minister twice, in 1783 and 1804. The cousin of Pitt the Younger, William Grenville, was created Lord Grenville in 1790, and he too became Prime Minister (1806). Four Prime Ministers, then, all related or related by marriage, and all intimately connected with Stowe.

The eldest son of George Grenville (PM 1763–65) was George Temple-Nugent-Grenville. He had been born in 1753, succeeded as 2nd Earl Temple in 1799, and was created Marquess of Buckingham in 1804. Earlier he had been a Bucks MP for several years.

His son, Richard, succeeded as Marquess of Buckingham in 1813. Then, to the surprise of many, he was created 1st Duke of Buckingham in 1822. Yet perhaps that surprise was not warranted. After all, he was great-nephew of two Prime Ministers, the nephew of another, and second cousin to a third! And family marriages had helped not a little also.

In those days it was the fashion that if a man married a wife who was heiress to great wealth, he added her name to his own with a hyphen. Thus the 1st Marquess of Buckingham had formerly been known as George Temple-Nugent-Grenville.

But perhaps it was carrying things a little too far when HIS son, destined to become the 1st Duke of Buckingham, lengthened his name to Richard Temple-Nugent-Brydges-Chandos-Grenville! When he inherited Stowe he became the largest landowner in Bucks and one of the wealthiest men in England.

But the great days of Stowe as a political powerhouse finally ended. Stowe remained a great stately home, but even that would later be challenged, and the house would pass from the hands of the Duke. Later, other quite different chapters in Stowe's history would be written. Meanwhile, it is a remarkable fact that in the 1820s no less than three Dukes, Buckingham, Bedford and Grafton dwelt in their great houses, all 'within a morning's ride' from Bletchley. And it is to Bletchley that we now turn to consider how that small town was to have its phenomenal influence on our national history in the 20th century just as Stowe had done in the 18th.

Bletchley Park

The Victorian Mansion could not be architecturally more different from the great house at Stowe. Yet what went on there during World War II was infinitely more far-reaching than the political machinations of 18th century Stowe. The meetings at Stowe had certainly been of national importance. The work at Bletchley Park was of world-wide import.

A whole shelf-full of books have been written about Bletchley Park and the astonishing code-breaking feats achieved there. Possession of the German Enigma machine, and the genius of the men and women secretly assembled there to master its secrets, enabled the Allies to monitor the thousands

Bletchley Park Mansion and its 55 acres held 'the best-kept secret of World War II'.

of signals sent out daily by the German High Command to all units of their Navy, Armies and Air Force. Bletchley Park, 'the best kept secret of World War II', may not have won the war single-handed for the Allies. But it certainly helped the Allies very materially not to lose the war.

The German Enigma Machine mastered at Bletchley Park. Thousands of German signals were read all through the war.

At its peak the Bletchley Park operation involved many thousands of personnel. They came quietly and settled in lodgings all over Bletchley and the surrounding area. If asked what they did they replied that they were 'working for the Foreign Office'. That reply had to satisfy their landladies. The men and women in 'digs' were sometimes called Guinea Pigs, because their landladies were paid a guinea a week to house and feed them.

The Bletchley Park estate was surrounded by barbed wire and was guarded by units of the RAF Regiment. To keep them alert and on their toes, officers told their men that if they failed to maintain proper security they would themselves be sent 'inside the Park', leaving unspoken the notion that Bletchley Park was some kind of asylum!

As well as in the Mansion itself, the work at Bletchley Park went on in a whole range of large huts erected in the grounds. Some distance away other, satellite units also operated, at Gayhurst Manor and at Hanslope Park.

Colossus, the world's first computer, built and used at Bletchley Park.

Only very much later would it be revealed that the world's first-ever computer was assembled and operated at Bletchley Park. 'Colossus', as it was called, dramatically speeded up the reading of electric punched-tape to 5,000 characters a second. Within a year other 'Colossi' were introduced which could read up to 25,000 characters per second.

Not Only In, But Out

If Bletchley Park was concerned with the RECEPTION of German signals, other places in the vicinity were concerned with the OUTWARD transmission of British signals. This outward transmission was of two kinds. One was the dissemination of propaganda. For this Woburn Abbey was the secret headquarters. There, the Stable Wing and the Riding School were adapted for the purpose. It was never referred to as Woburn, but was always called CHQ (Country Headquarters). The small hanger in the grounds, once occupied by the aeroplane of the late Duchess of Bedford, was used as type-composing room, manned by compositors from the Oxford University Press, Propaganda leaflets, typeset at Woburn, were taken for printing to HM Stationery Offices at Harrow.

Hugh Dalton, Minister of Economic Warfare, was made head of the SOE (Special Operations Executive). For a time SOE functioned at Chicheley Hall. At Woburn Richard Crossman was for some time head of the German Department. Dalton largely supervised Woburn operations through his secretary, Hugh Gaitskell. So in those war years three men who later went on to high political office, Dalton, Crossman, Gaitskell, found themselves engaged on secret war service at Woburn. All three later became Cabinet Ministers in Labour administrations, two of them as Chancellors of the Exchequer.

Side by side with the production and dissemination of propaganda leaflets, there was also broadcasting. Some originated from Woburn, but more importantly Wavendon Tower and Whaddon Hall were used. At Gawcott two 7.5KW transmitters were installed. A so-called 'European Revolution' station operated from Dawn Edge in Aspley Guise. Richard Crossman was also involved in this.

Sefton Delmer

It was Sefton Delmer who greatly galvanised the secret broadcasting. He operated from a secret house in Aspley Guise but made his actual broadcasts from Wavendon Tower. He conceived the idea of setting up counterfeit radio stations. The first purported to be Soldantensender Calais (Soldiers Radio Calais), and the second was Deutscher Kurzwellen-sender Atlantik (German Shortwave Radio Atlantic). For these a purpose-built broadcast station was constructed on a corner of the Woburn Estate at Milton Bryan, unoriginally code-named 'MB'.

Paris House

Another propaganda station pretended to be a short-wave transmitter operated from behind the Eastern Front. In fact it operated from Paris House. This remarkable mock-tudor house had been built for the Paris Exhibition of 1878. After the Exhibition it was bought by the Duke of Bedford who re-assembled it in the grounds of Woburn Abbey. Now, in World War II it was functioning as a secret radio station. (But not for the whole of the war. General de Gaulle lived there for a while. So did the Queen Mother's brother. Today it is a Restaurant.)

This has been a very condensed account of the secret work done both with inward transmission at Bletchley Park and with outward transmissions from Woburn, Aspley Guise, Gawcott, Wavendon Tower and Whaddon Hall. All these places are within a very few miles of each other.

Of course, much secret work was going on in many other places in Britain. But, given the supreme importance of Bletchley Park itself, it can surely be said that Bletchley, for a few years in the 1940s played a crucial role in our national history, far surpassing the different kind of influence its neighbour, Stowe, had exerted 180 years before.

Chapter 3

Things That Go Bump . . .

'The awful shadow of some unseen Power
Floats though unseen among us, visiting
This various world with as inconstant wing
As summer winds that creep from flower to flower'.

So wrote Shelley in his 'Hymn to Intellectual Beauty'. Did his 'unseen powers' include poltergeists? And, anyway, what is a poltergeist? The dictionary says: 'a spirit believed to manifest its presence by noises and acts of mischief, such as throwing furniture about'. And it goes on to explain that the word comes from the German 'poltern', to be noisy, and 'geist', a ghost.

One of the oldest streets in St. Albans is Holywell Hill. It adjoins the ancient monastery wall and Sumter's Yard, the 'tradesmen's entrance' to the Abbey is set in it. An early Georgian house on Holywell Hill was the location for poltergeist activity. Though the house was built in the 18th century, its cellars and foundations go back to the 12th century.

In the cellars were three aumbries, or recessed cupboards set in the walls. There was also the keystone and arch of what was once a passage, filled in long ago, which used to lead into the Abbey and to the tomb of St. Alban. It is possible that centuries ago pilgrims on their way to the shrine would pause for services in the cellars and that in the aumbries the holy vessels were kept for such worship.

During the war the house was owned by a man serving abroad with the RAF. His wife wrote to him relating the strange things that were happening in their house – knocking on doors, lights being switched on and off, electric bells ringing – all this with no logical explanation and with no apparent human agency to carry out these activities.

Such occurrences continued at intervals when the RAF officer returned after the war. The family became accustomed to the manifestations and developed an almost affectionate relationship with their resident but invisible poltergeist. 'Poltie', they called him (or her).

One day, after a fairly lengthy period without such manifestations the man was working alone in the cellar. Suddenly he became acutely aware of a 'presence'. He said: 'Good heavens, Poltie, where have you been? We have missed you.' After this the family continued to feel at ease with 'Poltie'. The householder said: 'He or she was very naughty really, but never spiteful, although he had me up in the night many times, ringing bells, turning on lights, and leaving doors open, particularly in the cellars. I wonder where 'Poltie' is now and whether he missed me when we moved away?'

Further down Holywell Hill in another house there was a rather similar 'visitant'. Here too the householders not only came to terms with their poltergeist, they even knew her name – she was Granny Sheldrake! They often heard her footsteps, and she seemed fascinated by electric lights in the house which she frequently turned on and off.

In yet a third house on Holywell Hill, it is said, the rather noisy poltergeist is a nun. She can be heard going up and down the stairs, or moving about in the cellars.

St. Stephens Hill House in St. Albans was demolished some time ago. While it still stood it had poltergeist problems. Doors opened and closed on their own, but always on the first floor. The last owner of the house said: 'When the house was full of people we did not specially notice the sound of doors opening and shutting, because it was a natural sound for a family house. However, when the family moved away and there was no one about, it was an eerie feature. But we accepted it as one of those things, and it was not frightening.

❖❖❖❖❖

It is easy to be sceptical about such tales. It depends largely on one's estimate of the credibility of those who are doing the telling. That being so, consider the testimony of no less a person than the Reverend John Wesley. Here it is:

The Rector of Epworth in Lincolnshire, and his wife Susannah, were much troubled by the odd things that happened in their Rectory. The Rector kept a diary and in it recorded 'An Account of Noises and Disturbances in my house at Epworth, Lincolnshire, in December and January 1716'.

The Rector was the Reverend Samuel Wesley. Both his two sons followed him into the ministry. They were Charles and John Wesley. And it was John Wesley who was so interested in hearing of the manifestations at the Rectory that he sought accounts of them from every member of the household. His mother, Susannah, wrote him long letters on the subject, and of course he had his father's diary as well. He collected and collated all these written accounts, and finally he published the results of his enquiry.

The manifestations began with knocking under the feet, groans and the noise of bottles being broken, footsteps and the sound of 'gobbling like a turkeycock'. There was a sound 'like the strong winding up of a jack'. The latches of doors were lifted up.

'One night', the Rector recorded in his diary, 'when the noise was great in the kitchen, and on a deal partition, and on the door in the yard, the latch whereof was often lifted up, my daughter Emilia went and held it fast on the inside, but it was still lifted up, and the door pushed violently against her, though nothing was to be seen on the outside.'

The combined effect of the testimonies of the Wesley family to the reality of what they experienced in Epworth Rectory would surely be hard to refute.

Music, Sacred But Strange

In Lambeth Palace Library they have the original manuscript of the music of the Missa Albanus, a setting of music for the Mass composed four hundred years ago by Robert Fayrfax (born

1470). He was the organist at St. Albans Abbey in the last years of the 15th century. He died at St. Albans in 1521 and is buried there. Exactly four hundred years later, in 1921, the then organist at St. Albans staged a performance of the Fayrfax Mass to mark the quartercentenery of the composer's death.

But the remarkable thing about Fayrfax's music is that on several occasions people have heard it being played in the Abbey during the night. On investigation, no one has been found seated at the organ. Two young men heard the music at 1.30am a day or two after Christmas in the 1930s. They went to the Abbey next day to enquire what the music was, because they had been impressed by it. They were told they couldn't have heard any music because the Abbey at that time had been locked up. And anyway the organ couldn't have been played because the engine-house was locked as well, so there would have been no wind for the organ. The two young men couldn't argue with that – yet they knew what they had heard!

During the war a Firewatcher on duty at the Abbey during the night heard the Fayrfax Mass being played. What is more, he claimed to have seen the organ keys being moved by invisible hands. He says there was a lighted candle in the organ loft, and before the High Altar he saw the Abbot and monks taking part in a great service.

A lady who moved into a house near the Abbey heard the music one night. She saw that only a single candle was visible through the window. She assumed it was just part of the Abbey's busy programme.

It maybe that so far this little catalogue of witnesses leaves one still sceptical. But if the testimony of John Wesley can be thought to give credence to strange poltergeist activity at Epworth, then maybe in the strange affair of the Fayrfax music at St. Albans the testimony of George Glossop should be quoted. He was a Canon of St. Albans Abbey.

He heard the ghostly music more than once. The first time was very early in the morning just after World War I. The Canon heard the music as he approached the Abbey. He wondered who could be playing at such an early hour. He let himself into the Abbey with his key. As he approached the organ the music stopped – and there was no one seated there.

The Canon next heard the music late at night. He was in his study at home working on his sermon. He heard the music very clearly but could not identify it. Three months later a performance of Fayrfax's music was given in the Abbey. Canon Glossop recognised one of the compositions as being the one he had heard during the night three months before.

Canon Glossop heard the ghostly Fayrfax music in St. Albans Abbey several times.

Finally, when that 400th Anniversary performance of the Fayrfax Mass was given in 1921, Canon Glossop realised that this was the music he had heard being played in the night time on those other occasions.

Artistically, one has to say that beautiful music in the small hours has more to commend it than the banging of doors and similar things that 'go bump in the night'.

❖❖❖❖❖

From Poltergeists to Ghosts

In a previous book, 'Eccentrics and Villains, Hauntings and Heroes', I mentioned 'Mother Haggy', explaining that I had been unable to discover more than her name, save that she was (is?) a St. Albans ghost. A chance encounter in the Great Hall of Durham Castle with a lady from St. Albans told me what I wanted to know.

It seems that in 1712 a little book was published called 'The Story of the St. Albans Ghost or the Apparition of Mother Haggy'. Mother Haggy was said to have been Mrs Jennings, mother of Sarah, Duchess of Marlborough. Apparently remarkable incidents followed Sarah's birth. On one occasion a hat, (yes, a hat), jumped into her cradle, turned into a coronet, and then shattered into a thousand pieces – a clear sign of the exalted but troublous life to which the baby Sarah would grow.

An alternative version of the Mother Haggy story said that she was not Mrs Jennings but a witch. This witch was able to appear from time to time as a ghost. More than that, she could vary her appearance as she pleased, sometimes taking the form of a lion, or a cat, or a hen. And she was capable of riding round St. Albans and up and down the River Ver in a kettledrum!

Sarah, Duchess of Marlborough was married secretly in 1677 to John Churchill, 1st Duke of Marlborough. It may be that the little 1712 booklet was really written as a political skit.

❖ ❖ ❖ ❖ ❖

At Claydon House, home of the Verney family, it has been said by some that a ghost appears from time to time – the ghost of Sir Edmund Verney, Royal Standard Bearer to Charles I. His arm, holding the Royal Standard, was hacked from his body at the Battle of Edgehill in 1642. Neither his arm nor his body were found after the battle so his grave is not known. His ghost, they say, has been heard at Claydon House as he searches for his lost arm.

Chapter 4

Witches and Witchcraft

Consider this heart-chilling statistic:

'DURING THE EIGHTEEN YEARS FROM 1643 TO 1661 SOME FOUR THOUSAND HAPLESS CREATURES WERE PAINFULLY EXECUTED FOR WITCHCRAFT IN BRITAIN.'

Those dates almost exactly cover the period of the Civil War and the eleven years of Cromwell's rule as Lord Protector. The statistic therefore adds an additional dimension of horror to the sadness of those days.

But it would be wrong to suppose that with the passing of Cromwell's rule and the restoration of the monarchy under Charles II, all was sweetness and harmony again, with no more drowning of witches. Confining ourselves only to our four shires, there are all too many examples of witch-hunting well into the 18th century.

Here is a shocking example from Oakley, near Bedford:

July 12th. A brutal instance of swimming a witch occurred at Oakley, near Bedford. An aged and infirm woman, over 60 years of age, was accused by her neighbours of practising witchcraft. The poor old dame, in order to free herself of this terrible imputation, consented to undergo the water ordeal. The parish officers, enlightened and public-spirited fellows no doubt, agreed to give this old woman a guinea if 'she could clear herself by sinking!'. She was accordingly prepared for the ordeal, tied up in a wet sheet, her thumbs and great toes bound together, her cap torn off, and all her clothing searched for pins – for a single pin, according to popular opinion, would spoil the operation of the charm. In the hands of the rabble she was dragged

'Swimming' a witch. The victim, with hands and feet tied together, was dragged through the water.

through the River Ouse by a rope tied round her middle.

Unluckily for the patient, but as might have been expected, her body floated, though her head remained under water. This cruel experiment, to the huge delight of the yokels no doubt, was made three times with the same effect.

As the reputed witch would not drown by sinking, a cry to hang her was raised by the rabble now thirsting for her blood. As the poor old woman lay half-drowned and helpless on the bank, she was most cruelly beaten, and would have been killed outright but for the advice of a humane bystander, who suggested as a crucial experiment that the mob should weigh the reputed witch against the Church Bible. The test was agreed upon, it being ingeniously argued 'that the Scriptures being the work of God Himself, must necessarily outweigh all the operations of the vassals of the devil'.

The Bible, which weighed twelve pounds, was accordingly brought, and the half-drowned old woman weighed against it. The old woman of course was heaviest, and she was dismissed, half-killed, as innocent. Many of the mob however considered this test irregular, and as they could not drown her, they wished to test her powers by hanging her. Luckily in this instance, the friends of humanity carried the day, and thus the poor innocent victim narrowly escaped with her life.

The next horrendous example comes from Hertfordshire:
April 18th. The town crier of Hemel Hempstead announces that 'on Monday next a man and woman are to be publicly ducked at Gubblecot near Long Marston for their wicked crimes'. The like notice was cried at Leighton and Winslow.

April 22nd. In accordance with the notice given by the town criers in various towns Ruth Osborne was ducked as a witch at Gubblecot. Both Osborne and his wife fell under the suspicion of the mob on account of supposed witchcraft. The crime of this poor old couple in the eyes of the rabble and the local Bumbles was possibly the fact that in their old age they had become chargeable to the parish. The Tring Overseers of the Poor, learning that the brutal and ignorant mob intended to impose the swimming test on the poor old man and his wife, made some half-hearted exertions on their behalf. The parish authorities placed them in the vestry of the church for safety, but this precaution was unavailing. The mob, raging for blood, burst open the door, seized the poor victims and abused them in a most merciless manner.

The accused were repeatedly dragged through a pond of water till the old woman died in the hands of her inhuman tormentors. A hulking rascal, who had acted as ringleader during the fatal outrage, actually went round among the spectators, and endeavoured to collect money for the 'sport' he had shown them!

The life of the old man was with much difficulty saved. Such a terrible outrage could not, of course, be winked at by the law, the more especially as the enlightened lawgivers of the day – and this occurred so late as the middle of the eighteenth century – were beginning to lift up their voices against the obnoxious statute of a grossly-superstitious kind. Three men were apprehended and tried for their participation in this frightful outrage. Two of them were acquitted, and the other, named Colley, was condemned.

This, and similar outrages in other parts of the country led to the abolition of the Witch Statute of James the First.

Finally, an example from Buckinghamshire, which, fortunately for the victim, had a happy ending:

February 28th. One, Susanna Hannokes, an elderly woman of Wingrave, was accused by a neighbour of bewitching her spinning wheel so that she could not make it go round and offered to make oaths of it before a magistrate. On which the husband, in order to justify his wife, insisted upon her being tried by the Church Bible, and that the accuser should be present. Accordingly she was conducted to the Parish Church, where she was stripped of all her clothes to her shift and undercoat, and weighed against the Bible; when, to the no small mortification of her accuser, she outweighed it and was honourably acquitted of the charge.

❖❖❖❖❖

In the Dictionary of the Bible and Religion Bishop Robert S. Ellwood writes:

'The charge of witchcraft was often aimed at "weird", aberrant, unpopular people, or people against whom the victim or victim's family had a grudge. In Europe the era of notorious persecution of alleged witches (was) a period of about two centuries after 1480. Estimates vary widely, but undoubtedly the number of people who lost their lives was in the millions and was mostly women. It seems beyond doubt that most of the elaborate witchcraft these unfortunate people were made to confess under torture existed only in their tormentor's twisted and misogynist imaginations. It is another example of the projection of evil onto the witch, in this case a deep-seated anxiety and social malaise engendered by Europe's wrenching transition from the medieval to the modern world.'

Witchcraft and witch-hunting were practised in England for centuries. A stern attempt to suppress them was made between 1645 and 1647 but with little effect. If anything, witch-hunts became even more hysterical than they had been in the past.

Professional witch-hunters appeared. They claimed to be able to determine whether a woman was possessed by the devil by sticking pins in her. Thus they discovered where she had been rendered insensitive by the Devil's touch!

Hopkins, the notorious 17th century Witch Finder, caused many deaths. But in the end he was himself found guilty of witchcraft and hanged.

The most notorious witch-finder was Matthew Hopkins who travelled all over the country with two assistants in the 1640s. Not all his victims were women. The Reverend John Lowes, who had been a Vicar for fifty years, was accused of being a witch. He was ducked, and was so badly beaten that he 'confessed', to avoid further suffering. He was hanged at Framlingham, having first been permitted to read his own funeral service!

Matthew Hopkins was finally himself accused of witchcraft and was subjected to the same treatment he had meted out to so many. He was hanged in August 1647.

In 1726 the Statutes against witchcraft were repealed but surreptitiously the ill-treatment of suspected witches still went on. It was not uncommon in country districts for charges to be brought for drowning witches up till the beginning of the nineteenth century.

Chapter 5

Out Of This World

Nobody knows who originated this expression. It is a 20th century vogue phrase and it means anything or anybody unusual. To be 'out of this world' is to be exceptional, special, original, 'one off', perhaps a genius, even a Boffin. And certainly an eccentric.

The village of Fawsley near Daventry gives us a good example of a man who was all of these things. He was the Reverend Dr John Wilkins and he was born at Fawsley in 1614. He graduated at Magdalen Hall, Oxford. After ordination he became a domestic chaplain. But soon mathematics and mechanics interested him as much as theology. He was one of the founders of the Royal Society.

When the Civil War broke out he sided with Parliament and was appointed Warden of Wadham. In 1656 he married a widowed sister of Oliver Cromwell, and in 1659 Richard Cromwell, the son of Oliver Cromwell, appointed him as Master of Trinity College, Cambridge. Thus far, his career had prospered.

But when Cromwell fell, and the monarchy was restored in 1660 the Reverend Dr Wilkins was dispossessed. However, he bounced back again and soon recovered court favour. He became Preacher at Grays Inn and Rector of St. Lawrence Jewry. From there he went on to be Dean of Ripon, and by 1669 he had become Bishop of Chester.

So he was a regular 'Vicar of Bray' sort of character, able to accommodate himself to the changes in religious views of those in power. (The original Vicar of Bray, in Berkshire, survived in his Vicarage throughout the reigns of Henry VIII, Edward VI, Mary, and Elizabeth. To survive, he had twice been a Papist and twice a Protestant. When he was accused of time-serving, he was said to have replied: 'Not so, neither, for if I changed my religion, I am sure I kept true to my principle, which is to live and die the Vicar of Bray'. He went on to be celebrated in the song we all know:

'And this is the law I will maintain
Until my dying day, Sir,
That whatsoever King may reign
I'll still be the Vicar of Bray, Sir.'

But the Rev. Dr Wilkins was not just 'out of this world' merely because of his ability to adapt to changing religious patterns. His real genius was that he anticipated 20th century discoveries and developments way back in the 17th century.

His mind was literally, as well as metaphorically, 'out of this world', because in 1628 he wrote a book called *Discovery of a World in the Moon*. In it he seriously discussed the possibility of communication with the moon by a flying machine.

In another book, *Discourse Concerning a New Planet*, published in 1640, he argued that earth is only one of the planets, and in his third book, *Mercury, or the Secret and Swift Messenger*, he spelt out how man could communicate with others over any distance. So in the 17th century John Wilkins anticipated by about three hundred years such marvels as space travel, moon landings, wireless and telegraphy. Truly, then, John Wilkins was a man 'out of this world'.

❖❖❖❖❖

Where Had She Been?

A Mrs Williams of Aylesbury claimed to have been literally 'out of this world' in the 18th century. In other words she was in a trance for a number of years and was supposed to have died. After her recovery she was asked where she had been , and what had she seen. She replied that she had been 'among the dead', but that she had heard a voice saying: 'Thou shalt not die, but live'. So live again she did, finally dying at the age of eighty-two in 1787.

She had always been a bit of a problem medically. As early as 1745 she complained of extraordinary fatigue. She was found one morning apparently dead. For three weeks she continued like this, to all appearances dead. But what puzzled everyone was the 'she did not become cold'. Some parts of her frame never did 'become cold', but no other sign of life could be detected.

They tried friction and they tried to administer vinegar. Nothing seemed to do any good. She still seemed dead, yet only parts of her 'became cold'. Then, suddenly, after three weeks she spoke! She was heard asking first for her leg, and then for her arm! Within six months she made a complete recovery – she had come back from wherever she had been. She was then about fifty years old and she lived for another thirty-two years.

But in 1787 she again seemed to pass 'out of this world'. Her second trance finally ended, as her first one had done thirty-two years before. It was then that she was asked where she had been and what had she seen. When finally at the age of eighty-two she really did pass 'out of this world', she left her friends and relations still puzzling over where she had been and what she had seen when she had been 'away'.

❖❖❖❖❖

A Curious Fraud

In the 13th century the de Montfort name was a name to conjure with. The de Montforts were Earls of Leicester. Some of the holders of the name and title were larger than life figures – the sort of individuals who might have been described a 'out of this world' if that 20th century vogue phrase had then been coined.

The first de Montfort, Earl of Leicester, took part in two Crusades, losing his life in the second one. His son, Simon de Montfort, was both a statesman and a soldier. He married the younger sister of King Henry III. Later he became the acknowledged leader of the Barons who wished to curb the excessive powers of the king.

In Hughenden Church in Buckinghamshire there is a Chapel called the De Montfort Chapel. In it are several monuments to members of the de Montfort family. Their stone figures show them with swords, and in armour, and with legs crossed as befits those who had taken part in the Crusades.

It is not perhaps surprising that such 'out of this world' characters are honoured in this way. But what is surprising is that such monuments should be in Hughenden Church. There is absolutely no connection between the de Montforts and Hughenden. Why, then, should Hughenden Church have a De Montfort Chapel?

Roscoe, in his book, *Buckinghamshire,* gives the answer. He writes:

'It has been conclusively shown that these monuments are spurious and were erected in the time of Henry VIII. The family of de Montfort had no connection with Hughenden. A respectable local family, the Wellesbournes, seems to have wished to make out a connection with a famous house. Hence this curious fraud?'

Perhaps if your name is Wellesbourne it is an innocent conceit to pretend to a well-born connection even if the claim is bogus.

Chapter 6

Dick Turpin – The Man and The Myth

A traveller dined with some Aylesbury gentlemen at a tavern. When dinner was ended the traveller left the room. He made his way to the stables and ordered his horse to be saddled. As he was about to mount his horse the landlord appeared. 'I'm off' said the man, 'I've left the reckoning for my dinner upstairs with the other gentlemen'. And away he rode.

The landlord quickly learned from the gentlemen upstairs that he had been bilked, and he was very angry. One of the diners urged the landlord to pursue the traveller, and offered the loan of his own horse for the purpose. The landlord accepted the offer and set off in pursuit. He caught up with the traveller within three miles and expressed his anger in no uncertain terms.

The traveller told him to calm down, and then said: 'Something tells me you have some Golden Boys in your pocket. I'll be glad to take them off you'. As he said this he produced a pistol and held it at the landlord's chest and quickly extracted ten guineas from the landlord's pocket. To complete the latter's discomfort the traveller then said: 'That's a good-looking horse you have there – it looks better than mine, so we'll make an exchange'. The landlord had no choice but to comply. As he rode off the traveller called over his shoulder 'Please give my regards to the gentlemen at your Inn, and tell them that it was with Turpin that they dined this evening.'

That was just one of the hundreds of tales told about Dick Turpin. The stories began in his life time and continued to multiply long after he was dead.

Among his many exploits, real or fabricated, there was the tale of how he jumped a five-barred gate and scattered his enemies in the process. At Loughton he visited the Old Swan from time to time. And it was there that he threw off his pursuers by reversing the shoes on his mare, so that they set off after him in the wrong direction! But at least one other inn, near Dropshort Farm between Fenny Stratford and Bow Brickhill, claims the same story.

The Olde Swan at Woughton, a reputed haunt of Dick Turpin. They say it was here he reversed his horse's shoes and fooled his pursuers.

Dick Turpin often stole horses, either because his own was exhausted, or simply to get a better mount. The London Evening Post in April 1737 carried this story:

'The famous Turpin who rides in an open gold lace hat, and his companion (who sometimes passes for his man) in a plain gold lace hat, were last week at Bedford and have since been seen at Market Street and Colney. Last Sunday they lay at a house near Whetstone, where Turpin left his dun horse and took away next morning a gray mare of the landlord's in its place.'

The London Evening Post carried story after story about Turpin. In May 1737 appeared this item:

'We hear that Turpin the notorious highwayman and murderer, after having committed several robberies on or about Epping Forest was luckily discovered by a higgler woman belonging to Bishop's Stortford, to whom he had given a bumper of brandy, and made her drink Turpin's health. After some conversation, and just before they parted, he told her that he was the man. She immediately gave information of him and described him and his horse. He was pursued five or six miles and then taken and committed to Hertford Gaol.'

But a few days later the London Evening Post had to correct its own story:

'We heard an account on Thursday night from Hertford that Turpin the famous highwayman was not taken, but on Tuesday last a person was taken up in the said town on suspicion of being Turpin, but set at liberty the same day.

On Wednesday last he appeared about the Forest; but it is imagined he has changed his road, or lies concealed. The report of him being taken was first raised by some relation of his, in order, it is imagined, for him to escape the more easily.'

Though the majority of Turpin's crimes were committed in Essex in general, and in Epping Forest in particular, he did frequently practice his nefarious trade in all the adjoining counties. At times he went ever further afield. He was by no means only a solo artist but was also a member of the Gregory Gang. At one stage he and other members of the gang, when the heat was on, contemplated on going to America. They got as far as Winchester but then turned back. At least once Turpin disappeared briefly to Holland, and tradition says he also travelled to Ireland.

Hero or Villain?

The accounts of his escapades multiplied and grew in the telling. Even allowing for the exaggerations, his skill, quickness of mind, and his horsemanship, cannot be denied. Small wonder that many marvelled at his exploits and thought of him as a hero.

The facts hardly justified such adulation. He was born in 1705 and was hanged in 1739. In the thirty-four years of his young life he had been butcher's apprenctice, cattle-lifter, smuggler, housebreaker, highwayman, horse-thief and murderer.

It has to be remembered that he operated in an age before there was an official police force. Sir John Fielding only founded the Bow Street Runners in 1748, nearly ten years after Turpin was hanged. All that authority could do to deal with lawbreakers such as Turpin was to rely on two ancient Acts or Statutes.

Hue and Cry

The first, Statute 13 of the reign of Edward I, was commonly called The Statute of Hue and Cry. The second, Statute 27 of the reign of Elizabeth I, was entitled: An Act for the Following of Hue and Cry. Both Acts required that when a 'Hue and Cry' was announced neighbours were bound to join in the hunt for the criminal up to the borders or boundaries of their district.

The almost total inadequacy of the system was so apparent that in 1735 an Act was passed to amend the Statutes of Hue and Cry. The chief effect of the amendment was that victims of highway robbery could claim from the County where the robbery took place the value of the money and/or articles stolen. Provision was also made for a Reward of £10 to be payable to anyone who apprehended the robber.

A Proclamation was published on July 9th, 1735 in the London Gazette, making special provision for dealing with crime in the capital. It read:

'By the Queen's Most Excellent Majesty, Guardian of the Realm of Great Britain: A PROCLAMATION *for putting in execution the Laws made against persons guilty of any murder or robbery in any street, highway, passage, field or open space in the cities of London or Westminster, or within five miles of the same, and for discovering and apprehending such offenders. Reward £100.'*

Turpin Goes North

Despite the fact that Turpin mostly operated in Essex and adjoining counties, it was in Yorkshire that he was arrested, tried and hanged. In the early summer of 1737 he had several near escapes from capture in Essex, and there was talk of increasing the reward for his arrest to £200. He decided to go north. Between July and September that year he carried out several robberies in Yorkshire and Lincolnshire.

At last he was caught and was sent to Beverley House of Correction before being taken to York Castle. And in York he was tried and convicted in 1739.

The trial was not as straightforward as might have been expected. For one thing there was confusion as to his identity. Was the man in the dock really Turpin? He persisted in saying that his name was Parmer.

And confusion continued after his conviction and execution. In 1740 a bookseller named John Newbury set off on a tour of England. In his travels he came to Leicester and visited the gaol there. His Journal recorded:

'At the Gaol we saw one John Clark who lay condemned for robbery on the highway. He told us that the person hanged at York was not Turpin, for he had robbed with him (Turpin) between Maidenhead and Colnbrook and other places in the last hard weather; that the person then hanged was an accomplice of his and Turpin's, and that they engaged that whichever was caught should take on him the name of Turpin; and that Turpin and he supported that man (named Parmer) in York Castle and was present at his execution; and that Turpin and he waited eight weeks to shoot a man in Epping Forest; but that Turpin was now living and had taken on him the name of Smith, and he kept an alehouse in the north of England.'

No doubt some were taken in by this tale but most people dismissed it as pure invention. Probably the nonentity, John Clark, produced the story as a way of identifying himself with the legendary highwayman whom he had unsuccessfully tried to emulate.

Black Bess!

There remains the most persistent legend of all – Dick Turpin's ride to York on his mare Black Bess. The story has been told and retold, in books and ballads, on the stage and on the cinema screen. Many generations of schoolboys have been thrilled by it.

In barest outline the story is that Turpin, having carried out a robbery in London, needed an alibi. He decided to ride the 160 miles to York in twelve hours. As soon as he reached York he went to a bowling green and took care to be noticed there. The Lord Mayor of York was present and Turpin made a great show of speaking with the Mayor and asking him the time. The Lord Mayor pulled out his watch and told him, and others standing nearby, that it was a quarter before eight at night.

The story is true in every particular save one. It *did* happen, but not to Turpin, and not in the 1730s. It happened in 1676! The true hero was a highway robber named John Nevison, alias Nicks, or 'Swift' Nicks.

It was the novelist, Harrison Ainsworth, who caused the story of the famous ride to York to be linked with Dick Turpin. His novel, Rockwood, was published in 1834. It helped to foster the notion of a romantic Turpin and of his noble steed, Black Bess. But it is now recognised that Turpin never made any such heroic ride to York.

Nevertheless, even if that legendary ride to York is denied him, many other of his exploits remain. He was a legend in his own life time, and has remained a legend ever since. That is is the reality, even after the myths have been stripped away.

Chapter 7

'Ex Africa Semper Aliquid Novi'

This phrase was originally a Greek proverb, quoted here in Latin by Pliny – 'Out of Africa always something new'.

Perhaps something that happened in 1689 at Middle Claydon qualifies as an example. In that year the Middle Claydon Church Register records that 'a Moor of Guinea' was baptised there. He was a little black page-boy employed at Claydon House. Not to put too fine a point on it, he was a young slave, though how he came from West Africa is not known. It was quite fashionable in those days in some great houses to have one or two young African page-boys. It is good to record that at that baptism in 1689 several members of the Verney family stood as sponsors.

A century later, and in Northamptonshire at Culworth, we find a stone near the church door bearing this inscription:

> *'Charles Bacchus, an African who died in 1782. He was beloved and lamented by the family he served, was grateful and humane, and gave hopes of proving a faithful servant and a good man.'*

He too must have been a slave. It is not known from which part of Africa he was, or how he came to be in the service of the family at Culworth. He was only sixteen when he died.

At Olney in Buckinghamshire is buried the Reverend John Newton. He had died in 1807 and had first been buried at St. Mary Woolnoth in London. His tombstone bears the following inscription:

'JOHN NEWTON, Clerk. Once an infidel and libertine
a Servant of Slaves in Africa, was, by the rich mercy
of our Lord and Saviour JESUS CHRIST
Preserved, restored and pardoned
And appointed to Preach the Faith he had long laboured to destroy.
He ministered near XVI years as Curate and Vicar
of Olney in Bucks and XXVIII years as Rector of
these United Parishes'.

The Newton Window in Olney Church, honouring the former Slave Trader who became Vicar.

Perhaps as remarkable as any other new thing to come 'ex Africa' was the conversion of that former slave-trader, John Newton, and the part he was able to play as a parish priest, to counsel and assist William Wilberforce in his long struggle to secure the abolition of slavery and the slave trade.

Later in the 19th century we return again to Northamptonshire, this time to Twywell. The Rector there in the 1870s was Horace Waller. He had been a missionary in

David Livingstone died on May 1st 1873 at Old Chitambo in the country now called Zambia.

Central Africa, one of the first to go out there with UMCA (The Universities Mission to Central Africa). UMCA had been formed in response to the challenge made by David Livingstone to the Universities and Church of England.

Horace Waller knew Livingstone and had been his friend, He was therefore saddened and shocked when he heard that David Livingstone, the great missionary/ explorer, had died at Old Chitambo in the middle of the country now known as Zambia, on May 1st, 1873.

Here I should declare a personal interest. In 1973 I was in Zambia. On May 1st, 1973, exactly one hundred years after Livingstone's death, I was present with many others at the exact spot at Old Chitambo where he had died. Also there from Scotland were some of the great man's descendants. All my adult life I have known about David Livingstone. I knew about Chuma and Susi, his two faithful African servants. When Livingstone died these two took an astonishingly brave decision. They determined to carry his body hundreds of miles to the coast and to hand it over to the British at Bagamoyo.

First, they cut out his heart and buried it under a great tree. (We stood under that same tree exactly a century later and paid our respects to the great explorer.) Then Chuma and Susi embalmed his body as best they could, using rock trade salt, and sewed it up in bark cloth so that it could be carried on poles by porters.

So began their epic journey – a journey which covered hundreds of miles, took ten months, and cost nineteen lives. They reached Bagamoyo at last and there they handed their precious load to British officers of the Royal Navy based on Zanzibar. Together with the body they handed over the

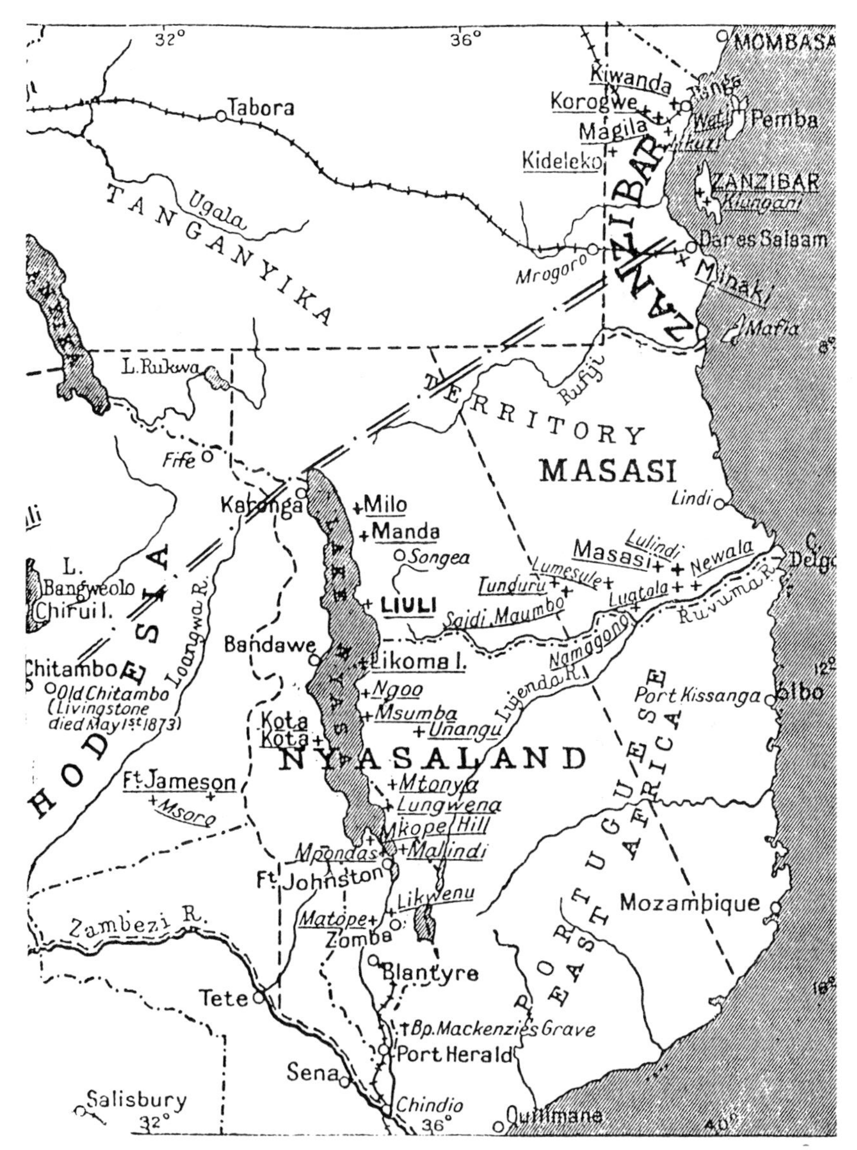

Chuma and Susi carried Livingstone's body through hundreds of perilous miles to the coast. Their route is marked =.=.=.=.

personal effects of the dead explorer.

To their great credit, the British Officers, recognising the extraordinary courage and faithfulness shown by Chuma and Susi, insisted that they too should travel to Britain on the British warship with the body of David Livingstone. So it came about that in April 1874 his two faithful African servants were present in Westminster Abbey when their master was laid to rest in the Nave.

The Author with Alan Paton in Lusaka, May 1959. Alan Paton's play, 'The Last Journey', dramatically captured the epic carrying of Livingstone's body to the coast by Chuma and Susi.

Meanwhile, at Twywell, the Rector, Horace Waller, was thrilled to give hospitality in his Rectory to Chuma and Susi. They stayed with him for four months and were invaluable in assisting Waller to sort through the Livingstone papers that they had carried so perilously all those hundreds of miles through the African bush. So it was from Twywell in Northamptonshire that the edited Livingstone Journals eventually went out to the world.

To continue declaring my personal interest, I should add that in 1959 in Zambia I learned that Alan Paton, the author of 'Cry the Beloved Country', had written a play about Livingstone's death and the carrying of his body back to Britain. He wanted the play, which he called 'The Last Journey', to be performed by a mixed cast and seen by a mixed audience. But in those 'apartheid' days in South Africa that wasn't possible. Greatly daring, I wrote to Alan Paton to ask if I could produce his play in Lusaka. When he graciously agreed I wrote to him again to invite him to come and stay with me. To my delight he accepted and he was present when we had the unique honour of staging the world première of his play, 'The Last Journey'.

In April 1874 Livingstone was buried in Westminster Abbey. Fittingly, Chuma and Susi were present.

Opening night was May 1st, 1959. Before the curtain went up Alan Paton performed the opening ceremony of our Waddington Community Centre. We played to packed audiences for eight nights. In the Coffee Bar we had the additional rare privilege of having on display priceless relics of David Livingstone - among them his pocket watch, his hat, a needle case, and his diary open at pages where Livingstone had written about Chuma and Susi and had recorded incidents which Paton had skilfully woven into his play.

'Out of Africa always something new'. The historic four months visit paid to Twywell Rectory in Northamptonshire in 1874 surely qualifies for inclusion under that head.

Chapter 8

'Benefit of Clergy'

In olden times English clergymen had the privilege of being tried by an ecclesiastical court instead of by a secular court if they had broken the law. This was known as 'Benefit of Clergy'. It was an advantage because punishments were less harsh in ecclesiastical courts. And in really serious cases involving an alleged murder, a clergyman would certainly benefit if he was tried by a bishop's court, because bishops could not impose the death penalty.

'Benefit of Clergy' was extended in the reign of Henry IV (1399) in two rather unexpected ways – to certain women and to blind persons. In the case of women it was laid down that no woman should suffer death in circumstances in which, had she been a man, she could 'plead his clergy'. In the case of a blind man, he could plead 'Benefit of Clergy' if he was able to speak Latin 'congruously'. To establish this, what was called the 'Neck' verse was invoked. The 'Neck' verse is the first verse of Psalm 51 which begins 'Miserere mei, Deus' ('Have mercy upon me, O God'). If a blind man was able to quote this in Latin adequately the judge would declare: 'Legit ut clericus' ('He reads like a clerk') and so the prisoner saved his neck. The same test would be applied to a sighted person who on the grounds that he was a parson could claim 'Benefit of Clergy'. He had to demonstrate his ability to read Latin.

By an Act of Henry VII (1485) 'Benefit of Clergy' was modified. It might continue to save the neck of a convicted cleric, but he would not escape altogether. He would be ordered to have his hands branded before release.

In June 1378 a certain Lawrence Thetcher found a dead man on the roadside. It proved to be corpse of the Reverend Willelmum Sapcote, the parson of Little Loughton near Bletchley. Enquires revealed that he had been shot dead by an arrow fired by another parson! This was the Reverend John Gervyes, the priest of the neighbouring parish of Great Loughton. John Gervyes fled to his own church for sanctuary. 'Benefit of Clergy' certainly saved his neck. He was fined.

An even clearer case of 'Benefit of Clergy' was that in 1368 of a Wolverton man with the remarkable name of John Garlekmonger. The contemporary records runs:

'Whereas John Garlekmonger of Wolvarton (Wolverton) lately apppealed John Okle of Stonystratford before the steward and marshals of the household and Thomas Frowyck, coroner of the same, of having, with others of 26 January in the king's 39th year, at Wolvarton in the king's presence within the verge of the household, broken the house of William Malyn of Wolvarton by night and stole 10 marks in gold and silver of the said John Okle was convicted of the said felony by the inquisition on which he put himself, but afterwards, on his alleging that he was a clerk, a book was delivered to him and he read thereon as a clerk, whereupon the said John Garlekmonger said that he had wedded a certain Mable, a widow, late the wife of Richard Gale, and was bigamous, upon which he was remitted to prison in the custody of the said marshals and by them committed to the Marshalsea prison until the king's court should be certified by the bishop whether he was bigamous or not; the king of special grace has pardoned the said John Okle his suit for the said felonies and any consequent outlawries and also the execution of the judgment which might be returned against him because of the said conviction.'
(Cal, Pat. 20 July 1368)

An earlier case had occurred in the same area when no 'Benefit of Clergy' could be invoked. It happened in 1279 and the case was tried in Stony Stratford. The record runs:

'Stephen Warkesdale of Bradewelle (Bradwell) struck Henry de Carynges, a man of Eleanor the Queen Consort, on the head with an axe stick, and Stephen Tebold of Great Lynford likewise struck the

said Henry on the head with a certain hatchet called a 'sperche', of which blow he died, and they both forthwith fled. Simon Tebold wished to strike the said Henry with a hatchet, which by accident escaped from his hand, and then he was taken and detained in prison in Aylesbury.'

The custom of 'Benefit of Clergy' had long lapsed by the time that the Rector of Tingewick killed somebody. He was the Reverend Mr Risely. It happened in June 1766. The circumstances were that Captain Fleming, ADC to the Earl of Hertford, was attacked and robbed on the road by a highwayman. The thief then rode off in the direction of Old Stratford. By chance, the Rector of Tingewick arrived on the scene in time to see what had occurred. The parson and the victim of the robbery both set off in pursuit of the thief. As they almost caught up with him they called on him repeatedly to halt. But the thief kept going. Whereupon the Rector of Tingewick, still galloping, drew his pistol and fired at the retreating thief. It was a remarkable shot, and the thief was mortally wounded.

In August 1766 the Rector of Tingewick was charged at the Northampton Court with manslaughter. Having heard the circumstances the magistrates acquitted the parson, to his great relief.

The Duke of Grafton was so impressed by the parson's courage (and his markmanship!) that he offered him the living of Ashton near Northampton.

So perhaps 'Benefit of Clergy' was not so obsolete after all!

❖ ❖ ❖ ❖ ❖

A quite different system of 'benefit to the clergy', though it had nothing to do with Benefit of Clergy as we have been considering so far, had to do with tithes. Here we go back far into pre-Christian history. Assyrians, Babylonians, Romans and Hebrews all knew and practiced the payment of tithes as a religious observance. The Christian church inherited the same custom.

As in other countries, old English law collected the tithes of the crops. Our cover picture, 'Peasants paying tithes', is by a follower of Pieter Brueghel and shows the practice in Holland.

In England, before the Reformation, the great or Rectorial tithes were generally taken by the monsteries, leaving the lesser tithes to the Vicar. After the Reformation the Rectorial tithes were often passed to Cathedral Chapters, Colleges, or Lay Patrons.

The process of commuting tithes began as long ago as 1600. Acts of Parliament in 1836, 1937 and 1951 carried the process further. By AD 2000 it is expected that all tithes will have been commuted.

Chapter 9

Tale of Two Doctors

It is fascinating to see in how many ways the careers of these two men ran in parallel. Both were famous physicians; both were Oxford men; both were academics, one being Sedlerian Professor of Natural Philosophy at Oxford, the other being a Fellow of Lincoln. Both moved to London and practised there with great success.

In politics they had a common experience, one being a great Royalist in the Civil War, the other being a Jacobite in sympathy when the Glorious Revolution of 1688 took place. So, in a sense, each had backed the losing side in their respective causes. Both were Tory in their political sympathies and both were loyal churchmen.

But the most interesting coincidence in their parallel careers is the fact that one of them purchased the Manor of Fenny Stratford, and the other purchased the adjoining Manor of Wolverton. So both impinged on the history of North Buckinghamshire.

One was born in 1621 and died in 1673. The other was born in 1652 and died in 1714. So while they were not strictly contemporary - one being born thirty-nine years before the other - their lives overlapped. How well Dr Willis knew Dr Radcliffe is uncertain. What is certain is that the younger man, Dr Radcliffe not only knew Dr Willis but held him in great awe and admiration.

Doctor Thomas Willis

Thomas Willis came of good yeoman stock. His great-great-grandfather was John Willis of Handborough in Oxfordshire. One of John's three sons was a Fellow of New College, Oxford in 1609. The next generation of the Willis family moved to Hinksey. Thomas Willis, the father of Dr Willis, lost his life in the Royalist cause, being killed at the siege of Oxford in August 1643. He is buried in Hinksey Church.

When his father was killed the future Dr Willis was a young man of twenty-two. He married Mary, the daughter of Samuel Fell who was Secretary to the Bishop of Oxford. His two brothers had close Oxford connections too. One of them, John Willis, was Chapter Clerk of Christ Church, and the other, William Willis, was a Fellow of Trinity College.

Dr Thomas Willis studied medicine and for fifteen years (1660–75) was Sedlerian Professor of Natural Philosophy. In 1662 he was one of the Founders of the Royal Society. The Society had in fact been established in 1660, but it was incorporated as the Royal Society in 1662. As its prestige grew Fellowship in the Royal Society became the most coveted honour among scientists.

Thomas Willis specialised in the study of neurological science and he was a pioneer in the study and treatment of diabetes, and in the anatomy of the brain. He discovered the 'Circle of Willis' in the brain and wrote notable books on his subjects.

But he was more than just a learned and academic expert – he was also a very caring physician. When he moved to London, where he lived in St. Martin's Lane, he soon earned a reputation as a compassionate doctor.

He was also a devout churchman and regularly worshipped at St. Martin's-in-the-fields before going to visit his patients. Whenever he had occasion to treat a patient on a Sunday he always gave the fees to charity.

Perhaps because he knew that his family descended from good yeoman stock, he took the opportunity in 1674 to purchase a Manor in the country. That Manor was Fenny

TWO

DISCOURSES

CONCERNING

The Soul of Brutes,

Which is that of the

Vital and Senſitive of Man.

The Firſt is PHYSIOLOGICAL, ſhewing the NATURE, PARTS, POWERS, and AFFECTIONS of the ſame.

The Other is PATHOLOGICAL, which unfolds the DISEASES which Affect it and its Primary Seat; to wit, The *BRAIN* and *NERVOUS STOCK*, And Treats of their CURES: With Copper Cuts.

By *THOMAS WILLIS* Doctor in PHYSICK, Profeſſor of Natural Philoſophy in *OXFORD*, and alſo one of the Royal Society, and of the renowned College of Phyſicians in *LONDON*.

Engliſhed

By *S. PORDAGE*, Student in PHYSICK.

LONDON,

Printed for *Thomas Dring* at the *Harrow* near *Chancery-Lane End* in *Fleet-ſtreet*, *Ch. Harper* at the *Flower-de-Luce* againſt St. *Dunſtan's* Church in *Fleet-ſtreet*, and *John Leigh* at *Stationers-Hall*. 1683.

The Title page of the first edition (1683) of Thomas Willis's book on Neurological Diseases.

Stratford. The opportunity offered itself because the second Duke of Buckingham was heavily in debt and urgently needed to raise money. This he did by selling parts of his estates. So Thomas Willis became Lord of the Manor of Fenny Stratford.

But on St. Martin's Day, November 11th 1675, Thomas Willis died and was buried in Westminster Abbey. So the Manor was inherited by his son, also Thomas Willis. The new Lord of the Manor took the opportunity to add to his inheritance by buying the adjoining Manors of Whaddon and Bletchley. The Duke of Buckingham, still being in need of money, was glad to sell the two further Manors to Thomas Willis.

A 1771 portrait of Browne Willis.

Thomas Willis died in 1699, aged only forty-one, and is buried in Bletchley Church. He and his wife Alice had two children, a son and a daughter. The son, Browne Willis, had been born in 1682. So he was still a minor, aged only seventeen, when he inherited all three Manors of Fenny Stratford, Bletchley, and Whaddon.

Thereafter the history of Bletchley and Fenny Stratford was intimately bound up with the life and character of Browne Willis – antiquarian, historian, author, devout churchman, church builder and benefactor.

As Lord of the Manor Browne Willis had the advowson, or right to appoint clergy of the parish in his Manor. This meant the ancient Parish Church of Bletchley, St. Mary's. Browne Willis had occasion several times in his life time to exercise this right. Being the cantankerous man he sometimes was, he quarrelled occasionally with those he appointed. The most notable appointment he made was that of the Reverend William Cole, the Bletchley diarist. At other times the living went to members of his own family.

In his other Manor, Fenny Stratford, there was no parish in which the Lord of the Manor could exercise his right of

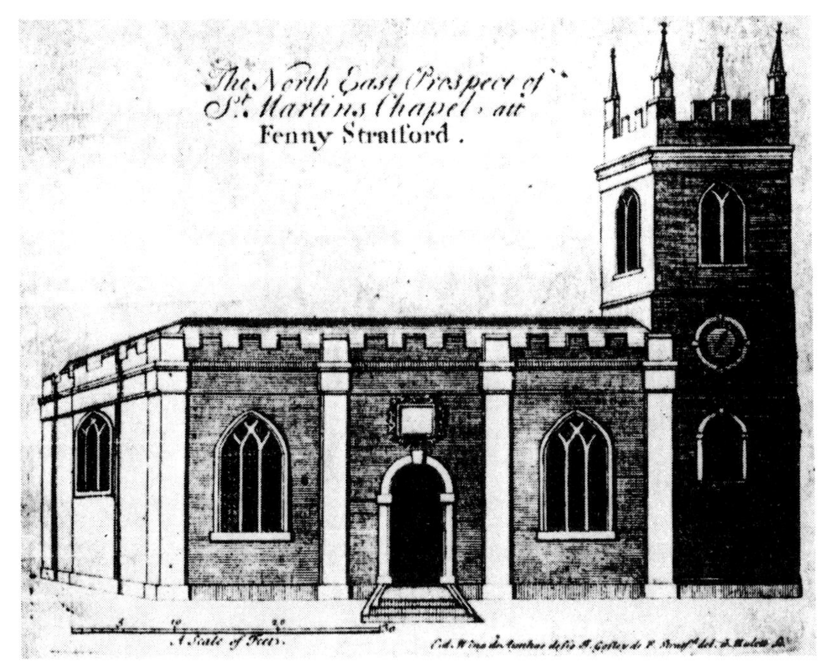

St. Martin's Church, Fenny Stratford as Browne Willis built it in 1730. It has twice been extended since then.

advowson. It became the most urgent and pressing of all Browne Willis's initiatives to rectify this. He built St. Martin's Church to be the Parish Church of Fenny Stratford in 1730. He chose St. Martin as the dedication out of the great veneration he had for his famous grandfather who had died on S.t Martin's Day. (By a strange coincidence his father had also died on St. Martin's Day.)

Browne Willis died on February 5th 1760 at the age of seventy-eight. He could have been buried in St. Mary's Church in Bletchley where both his parents were buried. He had been a considerable benefactor to that church. But, instead, at his known wish, he was buried in St. Martin's Church, Fenny Stratford. The building of that church, he once wrote, had been his 'chiefest and most real worldly comfort and happiness'. Attending his funeral were Burgesses from Buckingham, the constituency for which for three years he had been the MP (1705–1708).

Doctor John Radcliffe

A Yorkshireman, born at Wakefield in 1650, John Radcliffe was educated at the Grammar School in the town of his birth. He went on to University College, Oxford, graduating in 1669. He stayed on to study medicine and was made a Fellow of Lincoln College. He gained his first medical degree, MB, in 1675, the same year in which Dr Willis died. Thus qualified, John Radcliffe began to practice medicine in Oxford.

In 1682 John Radcliffe was awarded his Doctor of Medicine degree and decided it was time for him to move to London. His reputation in successfully treating smallpox cases preceded him there. Very soon he was operating a highly successful surgery in Bow Street.

Despite his often cantankerous manner, his medical skills and his genius for diagnosis made him very popular. Aged only thirty-two, his practice was not only large but it also began to include many patients of high rank, including royalty. In the following years he numbered among his patients Princess Elizabeth, the Bishop of London, Dean Swift, Sir Isaac Newton, and Viscount Weymouth.

In 1690 John Radcliffe stood for Parliament as a Tory and from 1690 to 1695 was MP for Bramber, a small village in Sussex. His wealth grew impressively. In 1690 his fortune was about £30,000. By 1707 it was over £80,000.

The 1680s was a very sensitive decade politically. In 1683, just a year after Dr Radcliffe moved to London, the abortive Rye House Plot failed to assassinate Charles II and his brother, the future James II. The plot had been hatched by men who feared that the monarchy would try to restore the Roman Catholic faith in England. When James became king in 1685 this was undoubtedly his intention. So a group of English Lords went across to Holland to invite William of Orange and his English wife Mary (the daughter of James II) to come to England and assume the monarchy. So the 'Glorious Revolution' of 1688 took place. King James II abdicated and fled to France. William and Mary were crowned and the return of Roman Catholicism in England was averted.

All this was of great interest and concern to the successful and popular Dr John Radcliffe, developing his medical practice in the capital. His sympathies were certainly with the deposed Jacobites. However, he took no direct action and as times passed he came to terms with the changed circumstances. Later, he even became Physician to King William III.

In 1706 he began to think of acquiring land in the country, partly for profit, but also for social recognition. In that year he purchased an estate at Linton in his native Yorkshire. He paid £14,458 for it.

In 1713 two events occurred which remarkably paralleled what had happened to that other doctor, Thomas Willis and his family. The first was that in 1713 Dr John Radcliffe purchased the estate of the Longueville family, Lord of the Manor of Wolverton – just as, earlier, in 1674, Dr Thomas Willis had purchased the estate and Manor of Fenny Stratford from the Duke of Buckingham.

Dr Radcliffe paid £40,000 for the Wolverton Estate. It comprised some 2,500 acres of good farm land, together with a number of dwellings in Stony Stratford, two Mills, and five of Stony Stratford's Inns. There was also the 'Great House', the former Manor House of the de Longueville family, though this was in a somewhat ruinous condition.

The second curious parallel between Dr Radcliffe and the family of Dr Willis was that in that same year, 1713, John Radcliffe was elected MP for Buckingham, the very constituency for which Browne Willis, grandson of Dr Thomas Willis, had been a member just a few years before (1705–1708). In the following year, Dr Radcliffe, the new MP for Buckingham, was appointed Deputy Lieutenant of Buckinghamshire.

Alas, Dr John Radcliffe had only a very short time to enjoy his new status as MP for Buckingham and Lord of the Manor of Wolverton. Within a year he had died of apoplexy, on November 1st 1714.

He had considerable wealth and his his Will he left a substantial part of his fortune to the University of Oxford. In

September 1714 John Radcliffe had decided the time had come to make a final Will and to incorporate in it the ideas and intentions that had taken a clear shape in his mind.

Statue of John Radcliffe in the Radcliffe Camera, Oxford.

The Will was finalised, and signed, on September 13th 1714. Its main provisions were:

1. The revenue from the Linton estate in Yorkshire to be used to fund two Medical Fellowships in Oxford; to give Advowsons to University College; to provide Annuities to several of his named relatives; to make certain annual grants to St. Bartholomew's in London; to provide funds for enlarging University College; and to build a new Library for the University. But the funding of this last large major project would only begin after the annuities to his sisters were no longer needed, i.e. after their deaths.

2. The revenue from the Wolverton estate to be used to make up any shortfall in the funds needed under 1. above, and thereafter to be administered by Trustees (named in the Will) for the effecting of 'such charitable projects as in their discretion the Trustees shall see fit to assist'.

So it came about that all of the great enterprises of the Radcliffe Trust over the next 260 years – the Library, the Infirmary, and the Observatory in Oxford – were largely supported out of the rents from the Buckinghamshire estate which Dr Radcliffe has purchased at Wolverton the year before his death.

The Radcliffe Trust likewise exercised a beneficent influence in and around Wolverton itself. It played its part in the development of the Canal, notably in assisting in the building of the famous 'Iron Trunk' aqueduct; it rebuilt Holy Trinity Church in what came to be known as 'Old' Wolverton, and built a new Rectory for it. (The Rectory, now known as Longueville House, incorporates some features from the ancient Manor House of the de Longuevilles which was finally demolished in 1720.) The Trust also contributed land and some finance to make possible the building of St. George's Church in 'new' Wolverton, together with a Vicarage. In 1994 St. George's Church celebrated its 150th Anniversary. The Trust contributed generously to the funding of the stipends of both the Wolverton churches. It gave land and funds to built St. Mary's Church and School in Stony Stratford, and assisted Calverton Church also. And over the years the Trust assisted in a whole range of civic and educational projects throughout the Wolverton area.

Holy Trinity Church, Old Wolverton, as rebuilt by the Radcliffe Trust, 1810–13.

When Dr Radcliffe in his Will directed how the Trustees should implement his wishes in Oxford, and thereafter embark on such other charitable causes as they should choose, he had supposed that the Wolverton estate would remain intact and continue to furnish the income for these purposes. In the event, circumstances beyond his imagining arose after his death to change the pattern very considerably.

First, the coming of the Canal, and then the coming of the Railway, both of these cutting right across the estate, and finally the coming of the new city of Milton Keynes, which subsumed the whole area of the estate – each of these developments undreamed of by John Radcliffe, made the selling of land from the estate inevitable.

So, by 1970 virtually the whole estate had been sold. Yet in a sense all of Dr Radcliffe's wishes have been handsomely fulfilled. His Trust duly carried out his wishes to the great benefit of the University and City of Oxford, and benefits in North Buckinghamshire have been effected too. Today,

280 years after his death the renowned name of Radcliffe resounds in Oxford where both Library and Hospital are named after him. And in Milton Keynes today The Radcliffe School is the title of the amalgamation of the former Wolverton Grammar School and the former Wolverton Secondary Technical School.

So, in their strangely parallel lives these two Doctors, Willis and Radcliffe, have played their parts nobly in the ongoing history of North Buckinghamshire.

❖❖❖❖❖

This chapter could almost have been called 'The Tale of *Three* Doctors'. Back in the 13th century a certain John de Gatesden bought Little Brickhill Manor. He was King Henry III's physician. His purchase of Little Brickhill Manor brought to an end a muddle about its ownership. The Manor had belonged to Stephen de Turnham. When he died his estate was left to be shared by his three daughters. But he also left considerable debts owing to the king. His eldest daughter, Maud, offered to settle the debts to the king on condition that she should be confirmed as owner of Little Brickhill Manor. Her sisters disagreed. The resultant confusion was ended when the king's physician, John de Gatesden, successfully applied for permission to purchase the Manor for himself.

So when Dr Thomas Willis purchased the Manor of Fenny Stratford in 1674, and Dr John Radcliffe purchased the Manor of Wolverton in 1713, both of them, unwittingly, were following in the footsteps of that earlier doctor, John de Gatesden, who in 1218 had purchased the Manor of Little Brickhill.

Chapter 10

Who Did Kill the Little Princes?

In a sense the story began in Stony Stratford. The year was 1464 and England had had a new young king, Edward IV, since 1461. He was tall, over six feet, and very handsome. And he loved to hunt. That is what brought him to Stony Stratford in 1464 – the hunting in Whittlewood Forest.

In the forest he met the young and beautiful Elizabeth Woodville, the widow of a member of the de Grey family. The de Greys were the most prominent family in the border countryside where Buckinghamshire and Northamptonshire meet.

Edward married Elizabeth secretly that year. Later their union was more formally solemnised. But not everyone was pleased. When royalty marries a commoner, however well-connected, jealousy is possible. In this case the unease of some was augmented because they found Elizabeth a touch too imperious and ambitious, and some muttered that her whole family was getting above itself.

The marriage itself was fruitful. Elizabeth bore Edward IV two sons, Edward and Richard. When the two lads were aged thirteen and eleven respectively their royal father died in 1483. In the ordinary course of events the eldest son could be expected to succeed. As that son was only a boy of thirteen, there would of course have to be a Protector. It was perhaps this fact which made it inevitable that rivalries would surface, and that criticism of Elizabeth, muted while her husband was alive, would become more vocal.

Meanwhile the two young princes were at Ludlow Castle. Soon they were brought to Stony Stratford, that very place where their father the king had first met their mother and fallen in love with her nineteen years before. The boys' uncle, Richard, Duke of Gloucester, hastened there on 30th April to take charge of the boys and to escort them to London where the older boy had already been proclaimed king. A date for his coronation had been announced – it was to be on May 4th.

This plaque in Stony Stratford High Street hedges its bets. It says Richard captured the young Prince Edward and that the lad was murdered in the Tower. But it doesn't say it was Richard who did it.

Today in Stony Stratford you can read on a plaque fixed to a wall the following inscription:

> *'This House was anciently the Rose and Crown Inn & here in 1483 Richard, Duke of Gloucester (Richard III) captured the uncrowned boy King Edward V who was later murdered in the Tower of London.'*

Shakespeare too, in his play Richard III, noted:

> *'Last night I hear that they lay at Northampton*
> *At Stony Stratford will they be tonight.'*

That play, Richard III, brings centre-stage the real subject of this chapter, and it asks yet again the question: Was Richard really the wicked uncle who murdered the little princes in the Tower?

Myth and reality have battled together over this question for the past five hundred years. There is a secondary question too – was Richard the physically deformed figure as he has often been portrayed? In his play Shakespeare had no doubts on either score. For him Richard *was* the wicked uncle and, yes, he was a hunchback. This certainty on Shakespeare's part has done much to fix these myths in the public mind.

Such myths and stereotypes are inseparable from historic characters. We all 'know' that Alfred burnt the cakes, that Ethelred was unready, that Richard I had a lion's heart, that King John signed Magna Carta (and lost his treasure in the Wash!). Perhaps William I was more fortunate – in his case the tag, 'the Conqueror', was kinder than his original tag, 'the Bastard!'.

Such myths and stereotypes are useful. They help us at least to recall the personages to whom they are attached. The trouble is that we may only remember the names, with their tags attached, and yet remain ignorant of the persons themselves.

In Richard's case, for centuries he has carried the reputation of being the monster who murdered his own nephews so that he could be king. And he has carried throughout the same period the notion that he was physically deformed and repulsive to look at.

Myths or realities? Any number of books have been written on the subject, and a Society exists which seeks to rehabilitate Richard III, to redeem his reputation and to free him from such charges. But it has to be noted that the most recent books on the subject have tended to the view that Richard *was* culpable, and that while he may not have murdered his nephews with his own hands, he did cause or authorise their killing. And the most inescapable facts of all are that in 1483 he *did* become king, and the two young boys *were* put to death in the Tower of London.

To take that second fact first – we have to wait a very long time for any proof to emerge. It was not until 1674 (191 years

The Tower of London where the two princes were murdered in 1483. But their bones were not found till 1674.

after their murder) that the remains of the two lads were found. It came about because workmen were employed to carry out alterations to the steps leading to the Chapel in the White Tower. As a result the skeletons of two young children were found. By then Charles II was king. He ordered that the bones should be translated from the Tower to Westminster and be decently interred in the Abbey. The urn containing the remains bears this inscription:

> *'Here lie interred the remains of Edward V, King of England, and Richard Duke of York, whose long desired and much sought-after bones, after above an hundred and ninety years, were found by most certain tokens, deep interred under the rubbish of the stairs that led up to the Chapel of the White Tower on the 17th July in the year of our Lord 1674. Charles the Second, a most merciful prince, having compassion on their*

hard fortune, performed the funeral rites of these unhappy Princes among the tombs of their ancestors, anno Domini 1678.'

But this did not end speculation. People continued to demand further proof of the fate suffered by the two lads. As recently as 1933 King George V bowed to public opinion and authorised the opening of the urn. Dr Lawrence E. Tanner, the Archivist and Keeper of the Monuments at the Abbey, and Professor W. Wright, President of the Anatomical Society of Great Britain, examined the bones. Their conclusions were that the bones represented the incomplete skeletons of two children – the elder four feet ten inches tall, and the younger four feet six-and-a-half inches tall. Using dental evidence they estimated that the elder child was twelve to thirteen years old, and the younger child nine to eleven years old. These conclusions exactly tie in with the known ages of the two princes. Further, Professor Wright said that the structures of the jaws and bones in each skeleton, indicated a familial link. He also claimed that a red stain on the facial bones of the elder child was a blood stain caused by suffocation.

The little princes were not the only ones to die. In quick succession Earl Rivers, the father of Elizabeth Woodville, and therefore the maternal grandfather of the princes, was murdered. So also were two of their uncles, Elizabeth's brothers, and Lord Lionel Grey. This wholesale removal of leading members of the Grey/Woodville family suggests that Richard feared their influence and needed to eliminate it lest it thwart his own plans. The effect in the border countryside of Bucks. and Northamptonshire can be imagined.

Take next the question of Richard's physical attributes. How really deformed was he? Sir Thomas More described him as:

'. . . little of stature, ill-featured of limbs, crook-backed, his left shoulder much higher than his right, hard-favoured of visage.'

Shakespeare makes Richard say of himself:

'I that am rudely stamp', and want love's majesty
. . . I that am curtail'd of this fair proportion,
cheated of feature by dissembling nature,

deform'd, unfinish'd, sent before my time
into this breathing world, scarce half made up,
and that so lamely and unfashionable
that dogs bark at me . . .'

Contemporary portraits of Richard offer conflicting evidence. While some do indeed picture him as deformed. X-rays taken of the paintings in the 20th century show them to have been altered so as to convey a seeming abnormality. The probability is that he did have some slight abnormality but that this was greatly exaggerated by his enemies. So the notion was allowed to take root that he had been a villainous hunchback with a withered arm.

Finally there is the greatest question of all. Was Richard a monster of a mogul? Did he murder his nephews or not? Many would say that five hundred years after the event it must now be impossible to know the truth. Others however have claimed that if modern judicial procedures were applied it should be possible to reach a verdict.

In 1984 Channel 4 put this to the test on Television. They staged 'The Trial of Richard III', re-enacting the events of 1483 and using contemporary sources. The verdict reached was: 'Not Guilty'. That conclusion was naturally welcomed by the Richard III Society. But it provoked a lively debate in the correspondence columns in The Times, showing that many still accused Richard of complicity in the murders, even if he could not be said to have carried them out in person.

The events of 1483 came at the end of that turbulent period of English history which we know as the Wars of the Roses. (See Chapter 16). It was a very fraught period as the protagonists of two factions, Yorkists and Lancastrians, fought for supremacy. In 1461 Edward had emerged victorious and became King Edward IV, ruling till 1483. His brother, Richard, Duke of Gloucester, was then faced with a choice. The dead king's son, Prince Edward, was only thirteen and could only rule through a Protector. Who should that Protector be? In that fatal year 1483 Richard had many rivals and many enemies. In the end he usurped the throne for himself and was crowned

Richard III. The boy of thirteen was disposed of in the Tower. His removal was necessary if Richard was to be king. It seems inescapable that Richard either saw to that removal himself, or caused it to happen, or at the very least, rejoiced that it happened.

Richard III ruled for two years and in many ways was an efficient monarch. But there remained one last episode of the Wars of the Roses. In 1485 Richard was defeated at the Battle of Bosworth. In that battle he lost both his throne and his life.

Chapter 11

The Rise and Fall of Bradwell Abbey

In about 1154 Meinfelin, Baron of Wolverton, founded the Benedictine Priory of St. Mary at Bradwell. To begin with it was dependent on Luffield Priory in Buckinghamshire but it obtained its independence in 1190. During the 13th century it seems to have been fairly prosperous and the building of the priory complex proceeded.

But the 14th century was a time of disaster. In 1349 the Prior, and many of his monks died of the plague. When it came to electing a new prior there was only one candidate, a man of illegitimate birth who in normal times would not even have been considered. In 1361 the Prior was much criticised for letting the buildings fall into disrepair. The poor man was probably handicapped by shortage of manpower. In the 15th century no names of priors are recorded between 1410 and 1490.

Yet the Chapel of St. Mary, which had been built in the mid-14th century, was developed as a healing shrine - no doubt with a view to generating income for the priory.

In 1504 the Prior, Thomas Wright, resigned. There were not enough monks for a time even to hold an election for his successor, though eventually one was appointed. The last Prior of Bradwell was John Asheby. It was in his time that the Priory was suppressed and made over to Cardinal Wolsey for the endowment of the new College he was building in Oxford. Bradwell was not alone in this. Its suppression was part of an Act for the dissolution of a number of minor houses.

On 27 July 1524 Sir John Longville, Patron of Bradwell Priory, signed a document assigning the Priory to Cardinal Wolsey. In return Cardinal Wolsey undertook to provide a chaplain to sing Mass continually for the souls of Sir John and his ancestors in the Priory church, or to have them prayed for in the College he intended to found in Oxford. The document also stipulated that while Bradwell Priory was being closed down and assigned to the Cardinal, the advowson of the Parish of Wolverton (today's old Wolverton) would be retained by Sir John Longville.

All this happened *before* the main Acts of Suppression closing all religious houses. The Bradwell suppression was achieved by securing Papal consent. It was part of Wolsey's overall plan for the founding and developing of new centres of education. In pursuance of this plan Wolsey secured the closing of some twenty-nine small religious houses in this way, for the benefit of new colleges which he sought to develop in Oxford and Ipswich. The Priory at Wing was another example.

To prepare the way for the dissolution of Bradwell Priory Wolsey ordered a detailed survey to be made of its buildings. William Brabazon was the Surveyor who carried out this task. He visited the Priory twice for the purpose, in 1526 and 1529.

Brabazon's Survey Report was very detailed. He noted which parts of the buildings were 'ruinows', and which would warrant retention. He described some buildings as 'fallynge downe', and others as 'in dekay'. He noted that some of the fishponds were now 'wasted and little or no ffyshe therein'. The pastures were little better, some of them being described as 'bereth no grasse.'

All in all then, Bradwell Priory was in pretty poor shape on the eve of its suppression. It seems clear that the decision was made to save the better of the buildings and to find new tenants or owners of them. The new owners would then adapt the buildings to suit their own purposes, saving and altering the most useful of them and pulling down the rest. Thus some priory buildings became barns, the Prior's Lodging became a farmhouse, and the Chapel of St. Mary was retained as the

Brabazon's careful survey in the 1520s makes it possible to create the picture of how it must have looked.

private chapel of the new owners.

Though centuries later so much has disappeared, the details given in Brabazon's Survey, particularly where he gives exact measurements, make it possible to recreate a fairly accurate picture of how the Priory was, both in its happier times and in its dying moments as a religious house.

While Cardinal Wolsey was the instigator of the suppression of Bradwell Priory and of so many others, his actions were at least motivated by the desire to create new places of learning.

But Wolsey's own time of power and influence was coming to an end. He finally fell from grace because of his refusal to support Henry VIII's desire to divorce Catherine of Aragon. In 1529 Henry VIII took the Bradwell Manor away from Wolsey and gave it to Sheen Priory, which held it for ten years. Sheen Priory was itself dissolved in 1539, after which, in 1543, Bradwell Manor passed to Arthur Longville.

Part of the Bradwell Priory buildings were then demolished and part of the site was used for the building of a new Manor House. Browne Willis wrote that Arthur Longville died insane in 1617, though it is not clear whether this Arthur Longville was the son or grandson of the one who acquired the Manor in 1543.

The Longville family were still living in the Manor in the 17th century. In the Civil War the estate was taken over by Parliamentarian troops and Thomas Longville was taken prisoner at Grafton in 1643. However, he was able to repossess his Manor in 1646 on payment of a fine of £800. And in the

The only surviving part of Bradwell Abbey today.

same year he was knighted by Charles I.

Sir Thomas sold the Manor in 1650 to Sir John Lawrence who in turn sold it in 1666 to Sir Joseph Alston of Chelsea who was created Baron of Chelsea and Bradwell Abbey. The Alston family remained in possession till 1716. During their time they enlarged the house by joining it onto some of the surviving medieval priory buildings.

So by the 18th century the House and the Park had become a quite notable property. But it was not to last. By the 19th century it was reduced to no more than a farmhouse.

Between 1919 and 1950 the farm was owned by Wolverton Co-operative Society. In 1971 the Milton Keynes Development Corporation bought it and made the farmhouse the Headquarters of its Archaeological staff and it became the home of the newly-established Bradwell Abbey Field Centre.

The small Chapel had survived throughout, though there were periods when it too might have been lost. It is there still, and now it is safe. That much at least then survives from the days when the Benedictine Abbey at Bradwell was home to the monks and their Prior. Continuing research and excavation may yet reveal to us an even clearer picture of how Bradwell Abbey once was.

Chapter 12

A Great British Hero – Myth or Reality ?

The king's daughter, Imogen, secretly married a 'poor but worthy gentlemen', Postumus by name. But her step-mother, the King's second wife, was determined that her step-daughter, Princess Imogen, should marry the step-mother's clownish son. In her rage at discovering the secret marriage the step-mother complained to the King and persuaded him to banish Postumus from the kingdom.

In exile in Rome Postumus boasted of the virtue of Princess Imogen. He entered into a wager with his friend Iachimo. The terms of the wager were that if Iachimo succeeded in seducing Imogen he would win the valuable diamond ring which Imogen had given to Postumus.

Iachimo was repulsed by Imogen, but he tricked Postumus into believing that he had succeeded. So Postumus instructed Pisanio his servant to kill Princess Imogen. But in his turn Pisanio also tricked Postumus. He provided Imogen with a male disguise and he showed Postumus a bloody cloth, claiming that it was proof that the murder contract had been fulfilled.

In her male disguise, as Fidele, Imogen became page to Bellarius and to two hitherto lost sons of the King, brothers to Postumus. They were living in a cave in Wales.

The disguised Fidele fell ill and was found unconscious by the brothers. They mourned her as dead. But Fidele recovered, only to find by her side a headless corpse! She was convinced, quite wrongly that it was her husband Postumus.

Meanwhile Postumus, still in exile in Rome, had been put in prison. A Roman army, led by the general, Lucius, invaded his home country. In the course of that invasion the general Lucius acquired Imogen (still disguised as the male Fidele) as his page.

In the battles that followed the Romans were defeated. The Roman general, Lucius, pleaded with the King to spare the life of the supposed page, Fidele. The King, who couldn't quite shake off the feeling that he knew Fidele, agreed to pardon him/her. He also said he would grant any favour that he/she cared to ask for.

Thus encouraged, Imogen asked that Iachimo (remember him?) be forced to explain how he came by that diamond ring. So the truth came out, and Postumus thus learnt of his wife's innocence. But he still believed her to be dead.

At this point Imogen announced dramatically that she wasn't dead! So the King discovered to his delight that his daughter still lived; Postumus rejoiced that he still had a wife; and to complete the all-round joy, the King also rejoiced at the recovery of his two lost sons. What joy, what rapture!

Was all this just a fairy story? Well perhaps it would better be described as a myth. It is based on a legend. According to that legend the King was Cymbeline, and his kingdom was Britain. Cymbeline, also known as Cunobelinus, was the father of Caractacus, and the king or chieftain of the Catevellauni. The legend claims that Cymbeline acquitted himself so well against the Romans that he was styled Rex Brittanicus, and was able to mint his own coins bearing that title.

The legend goes further, and says that Cymbeline's castle and place of residence were near the village of Great Kimble in Buckinghamshire. There, the name Cymbeline's Mount is said to be a corruption of the name Kimble.

So far we have merely recited the legend or the myth. Shakespeare knew of that legend and he based his play, 'Cymbeline', upon it.

But what is the reality? Well, Cymbeline Mount does exist and it is near Great Kimble and is sometimes known as Kimble Castle. *Perhaps the most interesting thing about it that it is in the grounds of Chequers Court, the country home of the British Prime Minister.*

It would be nice to think that successive Prime Ministers, strolling in the beautiful grounds at Chequers, can look upon the scene of triumph of a great British hero king who successfully withstood the Roman invaders two thousand years ago and ruled as Rex Brittanicus.

Alas, reality dismisses the myth. Certainly Cunobelinus (or Cymbeline) did exist, and he was the chief of the Catevellauni. But his headquarters were not at Chequers – they were at Colchester. And he didn't defeat the Romans.

What we still know as Cymbeline's Mount at Chequers was undoubtedly a hill fort, dating from two thousand years ago. But it was just one of several in the Chilterns.

Pity, really!

Chapter 13

Thank You, John Hassell

What do Daniel Defoe, Samuel Johnson, Celia Fiennes, William Harrison, William Camden and John Hassell have in common? The answer is that they all travelled throughout this country and wrote down their reactions to what they saw.

Daniel Defoe wrote 'Tour through the Whole Island of Great Britain' (1724–27) soon after Scotland and England united and when the Hanoverian dynasty was still young. Samuel Johnson wrote, 'A Journey to the Western Isles' in 1775. Celia Fiennes, in her twenties, made astonishing tours visiting every county in England in the 1680s. She did it all on horseback and she kept a diary. This was published in 1888 with the delightful title: 'Through England on a side saddle in the time of William and Mary'.

William Harrison was a 16th century priest and Canon of Windsor. He wrote 'Description of Britain'. His special interest was topography. William Camden (1551–1623) was an antiquarian and historian. He wrote his book 'Britannia' – in Latin!

That brings us to the last in the list, John Hassell. Only Celia Fiennes of the others had written of places of direct interest to our four shires. In this John Hassell joined her, for his book, 'A Tour of the Grand Junction Canal', published in 1819, dealt directly with many places in Hertfordshire, Buckinghamshire and Northamptonshire.

The Grand Junction Canal was decided on at a meeting in a Stony Stratford Inn in June 1792. It was cut from London to Braunston, a distance of forty miles, cost £500,000, and was finally opened for traffic in 1805. So, when Hassell wrote his book in 1819, though the Canal was no longer a novelty, it had had time greatly to affect the countryside through which it passed. When Hassell's book appeared the annual gross revenue of the canal was about £170,000. Some 1,400 people held shares. The current £100 shares were changing hands at between £240 and £250. The canal, then, was a success.

But Hassell wanted to do more than just write about the canal. He wished, he said, to combine the 'utile et dolce'. So his book treats of scenery, of observations on interesting places on or near the canal, of descriptions of some of the 'stately homes' nearby, and of some of the unusual people and events he discovered during his Tour. He never failed to comment on the churches and their architecture; and he looked back over England's long history, to the days when the Romans came; and he wrote of some of the early British chieftains whom they encountered.

Best of all, John Hassell was an artist. So his book contained some two dozen delightful water colours. These greatly enhance the books's attraction, and it is fascinating to stand with one's camera today where he once stood or sat with his sketch pad, and to photograph now what he once viewed. So, thank you, John Hassell.

We can begin with John Hassell at Watford. Already in 1819 he was obliged to write of it: 'Of late years it has become a place of considerable traffic and thoroughfare'. But for him its interest was that 'it is said to have been the residence of the Mercian Kings during the Saxon Heptarchy, till Offa gave it to the monastery of St. Albans'. He reckoned that Watford was the ancient residence of 'the renowned British general Cassivellaunus', and he devotes much space to writing of Cassiobury and its strategic importance against the Romans. In Hassell's day Cassiobury Park belonged to the Earl of Clarendon who welcomed the passage of the canal through his estates. For this Hassell praised him, and in contrast he blamed other short-sighted landowners who resisted 'this great national undertaking'.

At Langleybury he delighted in the parish church, listing its historic monuments to Sir John Verney, Prince Edward, Piers Gaveston and others. He notes that King's Langley is so named because Henry III built a Palace there, and Richard II was buried there, but he was later translated to Westminster by Henry V.

Hassell was distressed at Berkhamsted to find that its parish church, when he visited it, was 'in the remorseless hands of Church Wardens and overseers, stripping the walls of their relics and causing a general mutilation of its antiquites'. This so angered him that he went on to castigate 'this abominable mania, called beautifying and repairing, . . . it may generally be considered as illustrative of the acts of modern Goths and Vandals, destroying the richest works of past times and substituting a daubing of whitewash to hide their barbarism'.

At Tring he learned of 'an atrocious occurrence' (for details see Chapter 4), but he also found there 'a Charity School for the education and clothing of twenty boys' and he noted with approval that twenty years before his visit a Sunday School had been started for eighty boys and girls. The chief employment of Tring's inhabitants, he found, was straw plait and the making of lace.

He describes Marsworth Vicarage as 'surrounded by a moat of deep water . . . bearing the external appearance of having been a monastic establishment'. And from Marsworth on the border he passed from Hertfordshire into Buckinghamshire.

Here he pauses to debate whether Buckinghamshire is so called because of its plentiful beech trees (locally known as Buccum), or because of its abundance of deer (locally called Buc). He doesn't presume to take sides in the argument.

Aylesbury ducks interest him. 'There are many curious tales related of the methods used for promoting the early hatch of these fowls, but certain it is, let the Lent Assizes fall as early as may be, the Judges who go this Circuit always have a supply of young ducks placed on their table'.

To the left of Mentmore Hill is Berrysted House, said to

have been the seat of Henry de Blois, Bishop of Winchester, and brother of King Stephen. When Hassell passed by it was a farmhouse belonging to the Earl of Bridgwater.

Leighton Buzzard, Hassell points out, is a corruption of Leighton Beaudessert. Here the regular crossroads from the two universities of Oxford and Cambridge pass, the distance from each being exactly eighty-nine miles, he notes.

And so to Fenny Stratford, to which Hassell is not overly kind – 'a small decayed market town' he calls it. He tells how Browne Willis built the church on the site of an old Chantry Chapel, laying the first stone in 1724. Then he goes on: 'Near to the church is the Market House, a sorry little erection'. It had been an already old building when he saw (and sketched) it in 1817. Today, 175 years later, that 'sorry little erection' is still there, in good condition. Nowadays it is a popular and flourishing Fish and Chip shop!

By now Hassell is well and truly on the Watling Street. Writing of the great Roman road he quotes Stukeley who once wrote:

'. . . it is the direct road to Rome, for take a ruler and lay it on a map of Europe, from Chester through London and Dover, and it makes a straight line with Rome.'

Next to Newport Pagnell, where, Hassell writes, three hospitals were founded in early times. One was endowed by John de Somerie in 1280 for six poor men and women. It was still functioning when Hassell arrived there. He says that it had been refounded by Anne of Denmark. She was the wife of James I, so the Hospital was renamed Queen Anne's Hospital in her honour. He also saw seven almshouses in the churchyard, built and endowed by John Rivis, citizen and draper of London.

Lace making again attracted his interest. 'There is scarcely a door of a cottage to be seen during summer but what is occupied by some industrious pale-faced lass; their sedentary trade forbidding the rose to bloom in their sickly cheeks. It has been said that more lace is manufactured in this town and its neighbourhood than in all the rest of England'.

Hassell's water colour of St. Martin's Church and Aylesbury St. in Fenny Stratford as he saw it in 1817.

This is how the camera sees the same scene in the 1990s.

After Stony Stratford Hassell came to Grafton Regis. 'It was our fate to pass on the day appointed by the Justices for the licensing of victuallers where we heard the confirmation of one of the most arbitrary acts that ever disgraced an individual armed with power; the recital of which would be too disgusting to our readers.' So the reader, his appetite whetted, is left to guess what was too disgusting for Hassell even to write about it.

Stoke Bruerne, Hassell's next stop, is now the site of the fascinating British Waterways Museum. He whose book gives so enchanting an account of the great canal and the countryside it traverses, would surely applaud the Museum's success in preserving for posterity the canal and its characters.

Until the Blisworth Tunnel was constructed goods were conveyed over the hills to Stoke Bruerne by means of an iron

Stoke Bruerne British Waterways Museum.

railway. To build the tunnel the Marquis of Buckingham employed a Mr Barnes of Banbury – a strong-minded man who was virtually illiterate. He made all his calculations in his head or from memory. He could do the most intricate accounts in his head but was incapable of committing anything to paper.

In Nether Heyford Church Hassell found a memorial to Francis Morgan who died in 1558. Five years earlier he had sat a Judge and pronounced the sentence of death on the unfortunate Lady Jane Grey. It was said that the cruelty and injustice of that sentence so preyed on the mind of the Judge that he became insane. In the paroxysms of his last illness he cried out incessantly; 'Take away the Lady Jane from me!'.

As his Tour neared its end Hassell came to Daventry. Here, he writes, a Priory had been founded in 1090. As the centuries passed the Priory grew rich – so rich that it excited the attention of Cardinal Wolsey, who successfully secured its dissolution by obtaining from Pope Clement VII permission to close it down. Wolsey stirred up five persons to provoke a dispute with the monks, making sure that the case would be brought to him for judgment. He was then able to exercise the permission he had obtained from Rome to close the Priory. Hassell quotes Stone who in Annals explained what happened:

'But of this irreligious robbery, done of no conscience, but to patch up pride, which private wealth could not furnish, what punishment hath since ensued by God's hand . . . for of those five persons two fell at discord between themselves and the one slew the other, for which the survivor was hanged; the third drowned himself in a well; the fourth, being well-known and valued worth £200, became in three days so poor that he begged till his dying day; and the fifth, called Dr Allane, being chief executor of these doings, was cruelly maimed in Ireland even at such times as he was a bishop.'

After Daventry Hassell's Tour was nearly over. 'We had now the gratification of knowing that nothing of any import had been left unnoticed in our whole route'. He could justly make such a claim. His small book is a delightful compendium of interesting observations, of factual explanations of what a canal is and how it functions, and of delightful word-pictures of rural scenes. The latter are evidenced in such passages as this:

'Remaining for some hours on this charming brow, and sketching every object that presented itself, we found most abundant materials; the harvest was getting in, and the loaded teams were passing in quick succession; the labourers in the wheat field, with gleaners following, were all in motion, where the corn had been cut down; on the other side of us, reapers were trimming down the standing crops in one field, while in another a fresh group were mowing of beans. Village lasses appeared in the returning carts bringing refreshments to the sturdy husbandmen, who with backwardly inclined heads were seen lifting to their parched lips the much longed-for grateful jorum.'

And, not content with such word-pictures, Hassell compounds our gratitude to him by giving us the two dozen water colours he painted on his 'Tour of the Grand Junction Canal'.

So, thank you, John Hassell.

Chapter 14

Great Hampden of Great Hampden Buckinghamshire's Famous Son

If television had existed then, and had been used to show Parliament at work early in the 17th century, there can be little doubt which two sensational incidents would most have astonished the public.

The first would have been on 2nd March 1628. On that day Parliament's work had been preceded as usual by Prayers, exactly as still happens today. Then Speaker Finch announced the King's adjournment of the House. This provoked immediate uproar. Members rose to their feet and yelled 'No!'. Sir John Eliot made himself heard above the din and sought to put a single motion to the House. But the Speaker refused to recognise him and repeated King Charles's command that the House should adjourn. Having said this, Speaker Finch prepared to rise to his feet and to leave the Chamber. Had he succeeded, Parliament would indeed have been adjourned, for no sitting is possible with the Speaker absent.

Realising this, angry members took action. Two of them, nearest the Chair, leaped across and forcibly held Speaker Finch down in his seat. Uproar continued, and one member, Denzil Holles, was heard to shout: 'God's Wounds! You shall sit till we please to rise!'. The House then went on to debate a motion that no individual should be liable to pay taxes not sanctioned by Parliament. While angry and embarrassed Speaker Finch was still forcibly pinned in his seat, the House passed the motion by a mighty roar of 'Aye!'. Then, satisfied, the House adjourned itself.

'Ye House of Commons' in the reign of Charles I. Angry members pinned the Speaker in his chair to prevent him from adjourning the Session.

The second sensational occurrence was on 3rd January 1642. On that day King Charles I defied the most ancient privilege of the House by intruding into the Chamber itself. He was intent on arresting five members who had opposed him. That most ancient privilege of the House laid down that no monarch should ever physically enter Parliament. Members were enraged that day when the King, accompanied by one companion, strode into the Chamber. The King looked round the House, and saw at once that the five members he wished to arrest were not there. 'So the birds have flown!' he said; and he turned on his heel and left the house.

Both these incidents would have astonished and outraged viewers if they could have been seen on TV in 1628 and 1642. In Parliament today both of them are commemorated in two fine murals. The affront to the Speaker's dignity was painted by A. C. Gow. The King's provocative intrusion into the House was painted by C. W. Cope.

One man who was at the centre of both incidents is the subject of this chapter, Great Hampden of Great Hampden. He was one of those five members whose arrest the King sought.

He must surely be the most famous individual in the history of Buckinghamshire. At the height of his fame he was said to be the most popular man in all England.

John Hampden

John Hampden was born at Great Hampden in 1594. He went to Thame Grammar School and then to Magdalen College, Oxford. In 1613 he began to read law at the Inner Temple, London. When he was twenty-five he married Elizabeth Symeon and in 1621 he entered Parliament as Member for Grompound. Later, he changed his constituency and became Member for Wendover in his native county.

James I was then king. Already there were problems between monarch and parliament. The King needed Parliament to vote funds for running the country, but Parliament had a number of grievances and was not happy to vote funds unless these grievances were addressed. However, neither party was anxious to push confrontation to the limit.

But when James died in 1625 and was succeeded by his son Charles, that reluctance to force the issue vanished. Charles called his first Parliament in June 1635. It voted the King £140,000 but refused to give him a life-time grant of tunnage and poundage, insisting that the grant be for the current year only. Tunnage and poundage was a duty or tax levied by weight on cargoes at ports or harbours. Parliament's refusal to grant this on a life-time basis was intended to force the King's hand in dealing with Parliament's grievances. The ploy didn't work – the King simply dissolved Parliament and said he would rule his kingdom without it.

But Charles I's need for funds was too pressing for him to maintain this stance. He called his second Parliament in the following year, 1626. By now, in his desperate need for finance, Charles launched a tax plan. Under this plan the King's assessors allocated to individuals a figure which each must pay as a forced loan to the Exchequer. John Hampden was ordered to pay £20. When he refused to pay he was imprisoned.

Badly advised by Buckingham, Charles had embarked on a naval attack on Cadiz. For this he needed finance. The attack was abortive, and Parliament was determined not only to resist the forced loan but also to impeach Buckingham. When Parliament met in February 1626 Sir John Eliot, advised by John Hampden, moved Buckingham's impeachment. Charles was furious and for a week he imprisoned Eliot. Commons stood its ground and published a Remonstrance against arbitrary dissolution at the king's wish. In reply Charles burnt the Remonstrance and dissolved Parliament. For the next eleven years he managed without one.

During that eleven years John Hampden, with others, was still pursued for payment of the forced loan and still refused to pay it. For a year he was imprisoned. Throughout the country people applauded his courage and his popularity grew. Meanwhile a new MP was elected for Huntingdon. He was Hampden's first cousin and his name was Oliver Cromwell.

Hampden and his associates – the Country Party, set to work to draw up a 'Petition of Right'. The most important elements in it were:

- No taxation unless authorised by Parliament;
- No imprisonment of any citizen by the King's command alone;
- No peace-time billeting of soldiers without payment.

Reluctantly the King ratified the Petition of Right and in return Commons passed a grant to the King for £350,000.

The impeachment of Buckingham was still being pursued but was overtaken by events – Buckingham was assassinated at Portsmouth. Strafford took his place as the King's right-hand man. He was a formidable opponent of Hampden and his associates in the Country Party.

Still desperate for finance, Charles next declared that Ship Tax must be paid by inland counties as well as coastal regions. Again Hampden refused to pay, and for this his popularity soared still higher. Proceedings were taken against him in Court. For Hampden it was argued that without Parliamentary authorisation, Ship Tax was illegal. For the King it was argued that the monarch's powers were absolute and should not be opposed.

The twelve judges of the Court finally handed down their judgment. The verdict was in the King's favour but only by the narrow margin of seven votes to five.

In April 1640, after an eleven year gap, Charles called Parliament to sit again. He felt obliged to do so because he was now faced with serious trouble in Scotland. Parliament met in that year twice. The so-called Short Parliament was in session in April and May 1640. The Long Parliament began sitting in November 1640.

It was at this point that Charles sought to arrest John Hampden and four other members. Parliament now passed the Grand Remonstrance. The King accused the five members of High Treason. But six thousand Buckinghamshire men marched to London with petitions on behalf of their hero, John Hampden.

The King withdrew to Hampton Court. The five members made a triumphant return to Parliament. It was clear now that Civil War between King and Parliament was imminent.

John Hampden as Deputy Lieutenant of Buckinghamshire recruited a Militia Regiment - the famous Green Jackets - and he put up £2,000 of his own money towards its costs. In other counties similar Militia Regiments were formed.

On 22nd August 1642 Charles raised his Standard at Nottingham. The Civil War had begun. A major battle took place in October that year at Edgehill. In June 1643 at the Battle of Chalgrove Field Hampden was wounded. On 24th June he died at Thame where he had once been a schoolboy. He was forty-nine.

John Hampden was buried in the church at Great Hampden. His family had lived there since the Conquest when Baldwyn de Hampden held the Manor. No contemporary monument was erected to John Hampden at the time of his death. But a descendent, Robert Hampden, placed a monument in the church to the great patriot in 1755.

And in the busy market square at Aylesbury there is the fine bronze statue by Henry Fehr. So in the County Town of Buckinghamshire the County's hero stands on his pedestal, sword in hand and with arm upraised.

John Hampden's statue in Aylesbury Market Place.

Chapter 15

Before and After Fegan at Stony Stratford

Nearly four hundred years ago a certain Michael Hipwell died. In his will he left a sizeable estate, together with two inns in trust. His wish was that his legacy would provide for a free Grammar School in Stony Stratford 'for scholars of the towne or any of the next towns'. The money realised from his will was properly applied to educational work but it proved inadequate for the serious development of a Grammar School. So the Trustees of that Hipwell Bequest of 1609 obtained permission in 1819 for the funds to be used for a Grant to the National School Society for the support of St. Giles School in Stony Stratford.

Who knows? Perhaps if Michael Hipwell's dying wish for the establishment of a Grammar School in Stony Stratford in the 17th century had been more adequately provided for, that school might have grown and developed,and have taken its place as one of England's public schools. Then, to Eton, Oundle, Bedford and Stowe, Stony Stratford might have been added.

A second chance for Stony Stratford to have a great public school came in the 19th century. A new Vicar came to Stony Stratford in 1859. He was the wealthy and energetic W. T. Sankey. He took the lead in a plan to build a new school at the north end of Stony Stratford. To make room for the school and its grounds over thirty old slum dwellings were demolished, together with the ancient Horseshoe Inn.

Fine buildings were erected on the site, and playing fields were laid out. In 1863 St. Paul's College was opened. The school flourished for the next twenty years. It had some two hundred pupils and it provided a good sound education. The curriculum included the classical languages, Latin and Greek; French and German were also taught, together with Mathematics and Science, History and English Literature. Discipline was strict. Chapel services and religious instruction were important parts of the school regime. Old Boys of St. Paul's College included some who went on to national prominence in several fields - members of the Harmsworth family in journalism, General Nixon who found fame in Mesopotamia, and George Grossmith who for a generation was the country's leading comic actor.

Sadly, the school changed hands. After the Reverend W. T. Sankey died, new proprietors took over St. Paul's College. The deterioration of the school was rapid and dramatic. Parents took their sons away and soon numbers dropped below the level needed for solvency. By 1895 the School had to close.

An 1872 print from The Graphic of St. Paul's College, Fenny Stratford. If the College had survived it might now be well into its second century as a great Public School.

So, again, who knows? If St. Paul's College in its fine buildings had been able to continue the excellent start it was given in 1863, it would now be well into its second century, perhaps as one of England's public schools.

Ups and Downs

The later history of those school buildings in Stony Stratford is a story of remarkable ups and downs. When the College closed in 1895 the buildings stood empty for about a year. Then in 1896, of all improbable things, the buildings became a cigar factory! That venture proved a total failure and so once more the buildings stood empty.

They had been designed and erected as a school, so the obvious purpose to which they should be put was as another school. Or, if not a school, then as some other sort of institution. So the buildings were put on the market and it was supposed they would soon find a purchaser.

But for four years not a single approach was made to purchase them. Then, in 1900, an offer was made. It came from a surprising quarter and, in money terms, the offer to purchase was derisory. The would-be purchaser offered £4,500 for buildings which had originally cost over £40,000.

The one virtue of that derisory offer was that it was, literally, the only offer on offer! So, as the buildings had stood empty for four years, the offer was accepted. The next chapter in this story would last for sixty-two years. Throughout that time the buildings would once more be thronged with young students.

J. W. C. Fegan

The man who made that modest offer to buy the buildings was James William Condell Fegan. He had been born in 1852, the son of a Civil Servant at the Ordnance Survey Office in Southampton. Until he was ten years old his education had been carried out at home by his mother. Then he was sent to a Preparatory School in Southampton. The family then moved to London and the young Fegan finished his schooling at the City of London School (1865–1869).

In 1869 J. W. C. Fegan entered the offices of a firm of Colonial Brokers in Mincing Lane in the City. He, and his parents, supposed that he was embarked on a career in commerce. The family were all devout evangelical Christians. One night, in 1870, young Fegan experienced a personal conversion, moving him to offer his life to God in whatever way God should require. Initially he had no idea what this might entail. But events unfolded to show him.

The background to what followed is Dickensian England – or more particularly Dickensian London. Slums, poverty, broken homes, and virtually no proper schooling – these were the lot of many thousands of young children in London at that time.

Fegan, by chance or providentially, became aware of the plight of these children. While still working during the day at the Mincing Lane Offices, he began to spend his evenings teaching at one of the so-called Ragged Schools. His health broke down and he recuperated at Bognor.

Back in London, he realised that his life's work was to be for and among young children. May 1st, 1872 was a significant date, for on that day with the help of friends he opened an Industrial Home in Deptford High Street. It was to be the first of many such homes he opened. Others followed at Greenwich, Southwark and Westminster. An orphanage was also opened in Ramsgate, so that sickly orphans from London slums could benefit from fresh air at the seaside.

In the 1880s Canada was a Mecca for emigrants. Canada would welcome any number of teenage lads to work on her growing farms. In 1884 Fegan took an experimental group of ten lads to Canada. This emigration plan developed into one of the most successful aspects of Fegan's Homes. It was complemented by opening a Farm and Farm School at Goudhurst in Kent.

In 1900 Stony Stratford came to Fegan's attention. There were two reasons for this. The first was that in 1900 the lease of the Fegan Home in Greenwich expired. The second was that for some time Fegan had dreamed of a suitable place in the country where his 'pert Cockney sparrows' would benefit from fresh country air. Someone drew his attention to the empty College buildings in Stony Stratford. He went to look at them, and knew that they would be ideal for his purpose. He knew that the buildings had originally cost over £40,000, but he also knew that they had been for sale for four years without attracting a buyer.

Later in his biography of J. W. C. Fegan, Dr Fullerton was to write:

'Designed as a school for the sons of gentlemen, the buildings were almost luxurious, everything was of the highest quality, and the whole had cost £40,000. But the school was a failure, the Insurance Company to whom the property was mortgaged had foreclosed on the estate, and it was difficult to see what use could be made of such a property in such a neighbourhood. In the spirit of what in the event proved to be divine recklessness, Fegan made an offer of £4,500, though there seemed scant hope of its acceptance. It was accepted immediately, for it was the only offer made, and a date was set for the completion of the purchase – June 25th, 1900. It seemed impossible to get such a large sum in so short a time, but by prayer and picturesque personal letters Fegan obtained all but £9 by the set day. That night, at a Praise Meeting, the balance came from an old Christian man living in an almshouse.'

From 1900 to 1962 Fegan's home in Fenny Stratford housed some 150 boys.

❖❖❖❖❖

It is interesting to notice how the work Fegan did for London Orphans was matched, on an even larger scale, by a contemporary of his, Thomas John Barnardo. They were born within seven years of each other, Barnardo in 1845, Fegan in 1852. Both were devout evangelical Christians.

Barnardo was an Irishman, born in Dublin. Like Fegan, he experienced a conversion in 1862. For some time he preached in the Dublin slums. In 1866 he went to London to study medicine, intending later to become a medical missionary. However, seeing the conditions in the slums of London, he made that his mission field. In 1867 he founded the East End Mission for destitute children in Stepney. Since then the number of Dr Barnardo's Homes in Britain and abroad has risen to over a hundred.

❖❖❖❖❖

From 1900 to 1962 Fegan's home at Stony Stratford accommodated up to one hundred and fifty boys at any one time. For many years the boys' schooling was provided at the Home. But it was decided by the Ministry of Education that they should attend local schools. Many boys went on from Stony Stratford to the Fegan Farm and Farm School at Goudhurst, and then from there to Canada. But when school-leaving age was raised from fourteen to fifteen in England this adversely affected numbers going to Goudhurst, and Goudhurst closed.

Other changes occurred. In Social Services circles opinion was increasingly turning to smaller homes, run more on family lines. A corollary was a policy favouring mixed age groups rather than segregated age groups. It was felt that the ideal pattern was for small homes, with both boys and girls, and with children of all ages. Clearly such a pattern was quite different from what had been established for many years in Fegan's Home at Stony Stratford. So other smaller, family-type Fegan Homes were opened elsewhere. And in 1962 Fegan's Home in Stony Stratford was closed.

What Next?

What would happen to the buildings now? For a short while they were taken over as a Roman Catholic Prep. School. But this was of short duration. In 1972 the buildings were purchased by an international finance company - Société Générale. The French-chateau-like Chapel, which has always been the centre-piece of the campus, is now a restaurant.

So, from school for young gentlemen, to cigar factory, to orphanage, to Roman Catholic Prep. School, to Finance Company Offices and Restaurant - the buildings in Stony Stratford have certainly not lacked variety in the one hundred and thirty years since they were first built.

Today the former Chapel has become a Restaurant.

Chapter 16

'Uneasy Lies The Head . . .'

Twice in England's history there have been civil wars. The first lasted from 1455 to 1485 and we know it as The Wars of the Roses. The second lasted from 1642 to 1649 and is known as The Civil War. The first came about largely because the King (Henry VI) was too weak. The second happened because the king (Charles I) sought to be too strong. The first was a struggle between the monarch and the nobles. The second was a struggle between King and Parliament. In both our four shires were deeply involved.

The Roses and the Broom

The Red and White Rose emblems were not the only floral badges. There was a third – the Broom. The royal dynasty in England from Henry II to Richard III is known by historians as Plantagenet. This is because Henry II's father, Geoffrey of Anjou, sported a sprig of Broom as his badge, and, in Old French, broom is 'plante genet'.

The Plantagenet dynasty split in rivalry into two factions. One, led by Edmund Duke of York, adopted the White Rose; the other, led by John of Gaunt, Duke of Lancaster, adopted the Red Rose. These Dukes were brothers, sons of Edward III. The rivalry between them led to thirty years of civil war, to many murders, and to shocking episodes of deceit and treachery. Buckinghamshire, Bedfordshire, Hertfordshire and Northamptonshire figured in all of these.

It is said that twelve royal princes perished, as well as some two hundred nobles, and over one hundred thousand ordinary folk. Shakespeare in one of his Sonnets wrote:

'Roses have thorns, and silver fountains mud;
Clouds and eclipses stain both moon and sun,
And loathsome canker lives in sweetest bud
All men make faults.'

He was not thinking of the Wars of the Roses when he composed that Sonnet, but he might well have been. It certainly captures the horrors of those thirty years of war.

Weak, Pious, and Slightly Mad

Henry VI was king from 1442 to 1461. He was a direct descendant of Edward III and of John of Gaunt, the Duke of Lancaster. He was therefore of the Red Rose branch of the Plantagenets. He had a reputation for piety but was a weak ruler. Whether or not his piety tended to religious mania, there is no doubt that his mental instability combined with his feeble rule made it clear that he was no longer fit to be king. A Lord Protector must therefore be appointed to rule the country. But who? There was no lack of rivals for the appointment.

In 15th century England every baron had what amounted to a private army. It might be only a modest handful of retainers or, in the case of anyone who held a large number of manors, it could amount to a force of one thousand or more armed men. Those who were Dukes or Earls were immensely powerful – a law unto themselves. John Aylmer, Bishop of London, once wrote:

'If there be any noble man dwelling in the country, either a duke, a marquess, an earl or a baron, he shall lightly have in his retinue all the cobs in the country . . . And if any matters be touching him, his man or his friends, whether it be a crime capital or "nisi prius" sent down for lands the case shall weigh as he will.'

If, as well as being a Duke and a very large landowner with your own army, you were a descendant of Edward III, then your claim to be the Lord Protector would be almost irresistible. Such was the case with Richard Duke of York. In

1454 he became the Lord Protector and his son was named Prince of Wales. So power passed from the Red to the White Rose. But the Red Rose Lancastrians were determined to resist. The Wars of the Roses had begun.

Taking Sides

All over the kingdom the larger landowners and barons threw in their lot with one side or the other. And lesser Lords of the Manor in their turn gave their allegiance to the leading protagonists of either the White Rose or the Red Rose. It was all a bit like Jonathon Swift's epigrammatic poem:

'Some naturalists observe, a flea
Hath smaller fleas that on him prey;
And these have smaller fleas to bite 'em,
And so proceed "ad infinitum".'

So the battle lines were drawn. On the side of the Red Rose were the Dukes of Somerset (the Beauforts), the Dukes of Buckingham (the Staffords), the Earls of Oxford and Shrewsbury, and Lord Grey de Ruthin, whose many manors included Wilton and Bletchley.

The Longuevilles of Wolverton and Newton Longville, and Humphrey Stafford, Lord of the Manor of Little Brickhill, declared for the White Rose of York. This adherence of Humphrey Stafford to the Yorkist cause was important. He had precedence over all Dukes except those of the royal blood, and he was one of the greatest landowners in the kingdom.

The Battles Begin

In 1455 came the first battle. It took place on May 23rd at St. Albans and resulted in a victory for the Duke of York, confirming him in his position as Lord Protector. In the battle Stafford, son of the Duke of Buckingham, was wounded and later died of his wounds.

Two more battles followed in 1460. The first was fought at Northampton. In it the Duke of York was again victorious over the Red Rose Lancastrians.

Last Minute Switch

Edmund, Baron Grey, Lord of the Manors of Bletchley, Simpson and Great Brickhill, had marched with his retainers to Northampton intending to support the deposed Henry VI. But at the last minute he switched sides! He now declared himself for the Yorkist or White Rose cause. This switch did not go unrewarded. Later, in 1463, when the Lord Protector's son had become King Edward IV, Edmund was named Lord Treasurer. Two years later, in 1465, he was created Earl of Kent. But that was still in the future.

Meanwhile at the second battle to be fought in 1460, at Wakefield, the Lord Protector was defeated by the Lancastrian army led by Margaret of Anjou, the wife of the deposed Henry VI. But although the Lord Protector lost the battle (and his life), his son, the future Edward IV, carried on the struggle and in February 1461 he defeated the Lancastrians at Mortimers Cross.

Second Battle of St. Albans

On February 17th 1461 the Yorkists lost again at the second Battle of St. Albans, but were still strong enough for the young Edward to claim the throne. In March 1461 he defeated the Lancastrians at Towton, near York, and he was crowned in London as Edward IV.

Ghostly Comments

So there had now been two Battles of St. Albans, in 1455 and 1461. In Chequers Street in St. Albans stands Battlefield House. It is said to be haunted in two ways. From time to time the din and noise of battle is heard. At other times the chanting of monks is heard. Close at hand is the great Abbey, and not very far away are the sites of those two battles. If the two sets of sounds are contemporaneous, one wonders whether the monks were Yorkist or Lancastrian in sympathy! Or were they, like the rest of the nation, split on the issue?

Little Brickhill

Between St. Albans and Northampton where that other key battle had taken place in 1460, runs the Watling Street. And on the Watling Street lies Little Brickhill. History books do not record a battle as having taken place there during the Wars of the Roses. But it is at least likely that a skirmish or two did take place there. To this day old field names there include Battle Hill, Little Battle Hill, and Fuzzen Battle Hill.

Edward IV

Edward IV was king from 1461 to 1483. His reign plunged Buckinghamshire and Northamptonshire into national prominence. As a result, at least four members of the de Grey family were executed, and the little Princes in the Tower were murdered. All this flowed from the marriage of Edward IV to Elizabeth Woodville in 1464, and the whole sad story is told in Chapter 10 of this book.

Warwick the Kingmaker

To the other battles in the Wars of the Roses which were fought on the soil of our four shires we must now add a fourth. It took place at Barnet in 1471. At that battle Edward IV defeated the Earl of Warwick.

The Earl, who belonged to the Neville family achieved his earldom in 1450. No other individual had so great an influence on the events of the Wars of the Roses as he. He has been dubbed Warwick the Kingmaker.

He championed the Yorkist or White Rose cause. It was he who at the Battle of Northampton defeated and captured Henry VI. He then proclaimed his cousin, Edward Duke of York as King. Later he defeated the Lancastrians again at the Battle of Towton. But when Edward tried to assert his independence Warwick switched sides! Now he joined the Lancastrians, and Edward IV was forced, temporarily, to flee to Holland. Warwick then restored Henry VI to his throne in 1470.

But Edward IV bounced back. He returned from his brief exile in Holland and led his troops to do battle with his former friend and ally, the Earl of Warwick. That was the Battle of Barnet in 1471. Edward IV won it and Warwick the Kingmaker was slain.

But the year 1471 was not yet ended. Edward IV went on to defeat Queen Margaret at Tewkesbury and to kill her son, Prince Edward. And to complete the sad tally, Henry VI was murdered in the Tower.

Having disposed of the Earl of Warwick, Edward IV reigned for twelve more years. When he died in 1483 his son and heir was a lad of thirteen, with a younger brother aged eleven. The thirteen-year-old boy was proclaimed Edward V in 1483 but, as Chapter 10 related, he was never crowned but was murdered in the Tower.

Exit the Plantaganents, Enter the Tudors

No king of England has ever occasioned as much controversy as Richard III. He was the last of the Plantaganets whose dynasty had lasted three centuries. A key monarch in that succession was Edward III (1327–1377). Of his descendants in the male line, seven were killed in battle, and five were executed or murdered. Truly, *'Uneasy lies the head that wears a crown'*.

Richard III's death was tragic. His reign lasted a brief two years during which he felt himself threatened by many enemies. The Duke of Buckingham, who had been his most powerful supporter, rebelled against him. Richard had him executed.

But a far more powerful foe was waiting in the wings. He was Henry Tudor, son of the Earl of Richmond. He was born in Pembroke Castle and was the grandson of Owen Tudor who had married the widow of Henry V. His mother was the granddaughter of John of Gaunt. Henry Tudor was therefore firmly in the line of Lancastrian and Red Rose tradition.

Yorkists often tried to kill him but he escaped all their attempts. For a while he stayed abroad in Brittany. On August 1st 1485 he landed unopposed at Milford Haven and joined the army at Bosworth. Richard III fought bravely at the Battle of

Bosworth on August 22nd 1485, but he was defeated and killed. So the last of the Plantaganets had gone. Henry Tudor was anointed and crowned as Henry VII and the Tudor dynasty had begun.

Chapter 17

Gone But Not Forgotten

A Galaxy of Grave Words

'Those who have improved life by the knowledge they have found out, and those who have made themselves remembered by some for their services: round the brows of all these is worn a snow-white band.'

It was Virgil who wrote that, but of course he wrote it much more handsomely in Latin. Gravestones, tombs, brasses and wall tablets are all reminders to posterity of past mortality. Here, garnered from our four shires are more than a score of examples of epitaphs and memorials, a galaxy of grave words!

Shakespeare wrote: 'Brevity is the soul of wit'. This can be true even on a tombstone. So Shakespeare would surely have approved of the inscription on a gravestone at Fineden in Northants. It simple says: *'Here lyeth Richard Dent, in his last tenement'*. Barton Seagrave provides another example of economy of words. It is a 1616 brass to Jayne Floyd. She was the wife of the Rector and he it was who wrote her epitaph:

'Here was she born and bred, here was she married,
Here did she live and die, thus was she buried,
This brass can say no more.'

Accidents and disasters are revealed in some epitaphs. A sad example is found at St. Mary's Church, Baldock, in Hertfordshire. Its inscription says:

'In memory of Henry George, son of Henry and Harriet who departed this life March 20th 1861 aged 10 years and 10 months.
'How soon I was cut down, when innocent at play,
The wind it blew a scaffold down and took my life away.'

In Keysoe Church in Bedfordshire there is a memorial to an 18th century stonemason. Its quaint spelling relates the accident which befell him, but from which he miraculously escaped.

'The Great God and our Saviour
Jesus Christ, who preserved the life of
William Dickens, April 17, 1718 when he
was pointing the steepol and fell from
the rige of the middel window on the
spier over the southwest pinackel; he
dropt upon the batelment and their broke
his leg and foot and drove down 2 long
copein stones and so fell to the ground
with his neck upon one standard of his
chear when the other end took the ground
which was the nearest of killing him.
Yet when he see that he was faling crid
out to his brother Lord, Daniel, wats the
matter Lord have mercy upon me, Christ
have mercy upon me Lord Jesus Christ
help me but now almost to the ground.
Died November 29 1759 Aged 73 years.'

So all in all William Dickens didn't do badly. He had that fearful accident when he was thirty-two and lived another forty-one years.

Another epitaph which recalls an accident is found in Weston Turville Churchyard. It is in memory of two brothers, James and Frederick Bates. They were drowned in 1868, falling through the ice on the mill pond,

'They sank beneath the frozen wave
None to rescue none to save
Tempted to death in sportive play
These brothers sleep on Jesus Day.'

Some epitaphs read almost like newspaper cuttings! Take this one, for example, at Long Buckby. It commemorates the Curate's wife and says:

> *'She was a lady of spiritual and cultivated mind and her death was instantaneous, arising from fright occasioned by a violent attack made upon her house door by three or four men in a state of intoxication with a view to disturb the peaceful inmates in the dead of night.'*

A more poetical example of an epitaph that reads like a newspaper account is at Iver. It honours an eighteen-year-old Midshipman, James Whitshed, who was killed in action in 1813. It describes his death thus:

> *'His Time was short, and yet that honour'd name*
> *Shall live in mem'ry and be dear to fame.*
> *NELSON, expiring, could have said no more*
> *Than he whose early death these lines deplore*
> *Leading his Band to Board his Country's foe*
> *Too true, Alas! was aimed the Fatal Blow*
> *The Ball had pierced the youthful Hero's head,*
> *But ere to Heav'n his gallant spirit fled*
> *His look display'd a Soul despising death*
> *He cheer'd his Men and with convulsive breath*
> *Dying exclaimed amidst the Battle's roar*
> *Carry her if you can, my lads. I am no more.'*

In All Saints' Church at Southill in Bedfordshire there is a plaque worded as follows:

> *'To the perpetual disgrace of*
> *Public Justice*
> *The Honourable John Byng*
> *Admiral of the Blue*
> *Fell a martyr to*
> *Political Persecution*
> *On March 14 in the year 1757*
> *When Bravery and Loyalty*
> *Were insufficient Securities*
> *For the Life and Honour*
> *Of a Naval Officer.'*

What sad tale lies behind these bitter words? John Byng was born in 1714, the fourth son of Admiral George Byng. He joined the Navy at fourteen. By 1745, aged forty-one he was Rear-Admiral of the Mediterranean Fleet and in 1756 was promoted as full Admiral. In that year the Seven Years War began. Admiral Byng was sent with a poorly equipped squadron to relieve Minorca which was being beseiged by the French. His squadron was quite inadequate for the task and Byng was obliged to withdraw to Gibraltar. The Admiralty blamed him for the failure and brought him home under arrest to stand trial. He was charged with cowardice and disaffection but was acquitted on both counts. Nevertheless the Court Martial found him guilty of neglect of duty and ordered his execution. The harsh sentence was carried out on HMS Monarque at Portsmouth. Many regarded this as 'judicial murder' and the bitter words on the memorial at Southill reflect this.

Syresham provides another sad example of a dark deed done in a past age. It is the memorial in the Wesleyan Chapel to a village martyr, John Kurde. He was a shoemaker of little education but great faith. He was persecuted for that faith in the 16th century when he was arrested and taken to Northampton where he was imprisoned in the Castle. Finally he was burned to death in the stone quarry at the gate of the town. His inscription runs:

> *'In memory of John Kurde, shoemaker, the Syresham Martyr, burnt at the stake in defence of the truth, 1557. Tell ye your children of it, and let your children tell their children, and their children another generation.'*

In contrast are the many epitaphs which pay tribute to the memory of a happy marriage. A good example is found on a brass to Sir Robert Pemberton in Rushden Church. Sir Robert was a Gentleman Usher to Elizabeth I. His monument shows him with his wife and their four sons and four daughters, together with these words:

> *'By God's grace we so evenly were paired*
> *As that in sexes equally we shared.*

We had eight children to augment our joys
For her four daughters and for me four boys.'

Some epitaphs are cryptic in the extreme, leaving the reader puzzled. Courteenhall in Northamptonshire has a prime example. The black marble tomb of Sir Richard Ouseley has this strange inscription:

'A Salop's Ouseley I, a ruen Partrige woone,
No birds I had her by; such work with her was doone.
Shee dead I turtle sought, A Wake in Salsie bred.
Twice six birds shee me brought, she lys but I am dead.
But when ninth year was come, I sleapt that was a-Wake
So, yielding to Death's doome, did here my lodging take.'

Puzzled? Well, here is the explanation. Richard Ouseley came from Shrewsbury (Salop). His first wife was a Partridge but she bore him no children. His second wife was a Wake, who came from Salcey. She bore him twelve children. The reader further needs to understand that the first four lines are the words of the husband; the last two lines are to be understood as spoken by the wife, who died nine years after her husband.

Upton-cum-Chalvey has a cryptic epitaph too. On a flat tombstone there are the words:

'Here lies the body of Sarah Bramstone
of Eton, Spinster, a person who dared to be just in the
reign of George II.'

Memorials to the very young are naturally touching. Chicheley Church has a memorial to John, the son of Sir Anthony and Lady Chester who died at the age of three in 1640. It is inscribed on a slate in the floor and the feet of countless people in the more than three centuries since he was laid to rest have largely obliterated the wording. However, earlier historians have preserved the wording, which is:

'Griv'd at the world and crimes, this early bloome
Look'd round and sigh'd, & stole into his tombe.
His fall was like his birth, too q'ck this rose
Made hastee to spread, and the same hast to close.
Here lies his dust, but his best tomb's fled hence
For marle cannot last like innocence.'

Chicheley Church has a very sad memorial to a three-year-old boy. He died in 1640.

Walton Church (now part of the buildings of the Open University) also has a quaint and touching monument to a child. She was Elizabeth Pyxe who died in 1616 aged eleven. Part of the inscription is in Latin, but two verses are in English. The first runs:

'Elizabeth the daughter deare
of William Pyxe heere lies interr'd
O! that her death for many a yeare
Almighty God would have deferr'd.'

There is a touching quaintness about a memorial at Marlow. In the 18th century John Richardson amassed a great fortune as a strolling player. According to Lipscomb Richardson paid

1,000 guineas to buy an infant who was 'black and white spotted'. He exhibited him to the public as a spectacle and curiosity. But he was solicitous for the freakish child's welfare and had him baptised at Newington in Surrey. He also arranged some education for the child. But in 1812 the child died at the age of eight and was buried in the churchyard at Marlow. Lipscomb writes of a gravestone with a long inscription and he pays tribute to Richardson's 'munificence and affection' towards the child. In his will Richardson asked that he should be buried in the same grave as the little 'black and white spotted' boy.

Here are two epitaphs which remind us that acute differences in life cease to divide after death. The first is at Blatherwycke Church in Northamptonshire. Sir Humphrey Stafford built Elizabeth Hall in that place and his family's monuments are in the church. One of his relatives was killed in Jack Cade's Rebellion. Another was beheaded in Lord Lovell's insurrection. A third relative, Thomas Randolph, died in 1635. His epitaph contains the words:

'Here sleep thirteen together in one tomb
And all these great yet quarrel not for room.'

Even more dramatically the same point is made in the very long inscription outside Hardwick Church. This records the fact that the remains of no less than two hundred and forty seven men are buried nearby. They had all been killed in the Civil War battle at Holmans Bridge near Aylesbury in 1642. The remains of the fallen had only been rediscovered in 1818. They were both Cavaliers and Roundheads, indistinguishable in death. So, reverently re-interred, the enemies share a common grave. The long inscription to their memory concludes:

'May the memory of the brave be respected and may our
country never again be called to take part in contests such
as these which this tablet records.'

It must be very rare for anyone to erect a memorial to himself before he has even died! But Thomas Tipping of Ickford did exactly that in 1595 several years before he actually died. His monument, besides recording his death (before it happened) also commemorated his 'chaste wife' and their nine children. They are all there to be seen on a black marble column, in suitably graduated sizes, each with their christian names over their respective heads.

No doubt there is a deep moral lesson to be learned from the unique Rose Brass in Edlesborough Church. But what is it? The words are:

'What I spent I had,
What I gave I have,
What I refused I am being punished for,
What I kept I have lost.'

Francis Quarles was Poet-Laureate to James I. His sister married Sir Cope Doyley. When she died the poet composed her epitaph for the monument in Hambleden Church. In it he related Lady Doyley's virtues by comparing her to no less than eight of the most notable women in scripture:

'In spirit a Jael,
Rebecca in grace, in heart an Abigail;
In works a Dorcas, to the church a Hannah,
And to her spouse, Susannah,
Prudently simple, providentially wary
To the world a Martha, and to Heaven a Mary.'

In Hughenden Church a simple marble tablet pays a royal tribute. It says:

'To the dear and honoured memory of Benjamin Disraeli
Earl of Beaconsfield
this memorial is placed by his grateful and affectionate
Sovereign and friend, Victoria R.I.
"Kings love him that speaketh right" Proverbs xvi.13
Feb.27th, 1882.'

Higham Gobion in Bedfordshire had a very learned Rector in the 17th century. His name was Edward Castell who died, aged eighty, on January 5th 1685. He was a great linguist and compiled a Lexicon Heptaglotten – in other words a dictionary for seven languages. The languages were Hebrew, Chaldee, Syriac, Samaritan, Ethiopic, Arabic and Persian. He published his great work at his own expense, but three hundred copies

The unique memorial in Hughenden Church from the Sovereign to her friend, Disraeli.

were destroyed in a great fire in London in 1686, with a further two hundred copies spoiled. He bequeathed one hundred copies to the Bishop of London. When he died he was buried at Higham Gobion. He had composed his own epitaph and it was duly inscribed on his tomb. It is in Arabic. Translated into English it says: *'Living here he chose to be buried in hopes of a better place than this'.*

Chapter 18

The Other Fawkes

Everyone knows about Guy Fawkes. He is the man who tried to blow up Parliament in 1605. His infamy has fixed him in our Calendar as well as in our memory - each year on November 5th we celebrate Guy Fawkes Night.

But there was an earlier Fawkes, less well known but a remarkable man. This other Fawkes was of special significance to Bedfordshire, but he also loomed large in national affairs. There were periods when he could almost be said to be running the country. Yet he was not an Englishman.

Fawkes de Breaute was born at Poitou in France. He was a professional soldier, ready to serve for anyone who would pay for his services. It was this fact that brought him to England.

King Richard I - the Lionheart - had died. He was succeeded in 1199 by his brother John. King John was soon in trouble. Though an able man, he was erratic and domineering. He lost Normandy, which from the time of William the Conqueror had been ruled as part of the English kingdom; he quarrelled with the Pope; and there were ominous signs that he would soon have trouble with the Barons. That trouble was to culminate in 1215 in the confrontation at Runnemede when John was forced to sign the Magna Carta.

King John relied increasingly on paid soldiers, or mercenaries. Many of these he recruited overseas. Fawkes de Breaute was one of them. In his service to King John Fawkes headed a successful campaign in Wales in 1211.

At the beginning of 1215 the Barons were getting organised,

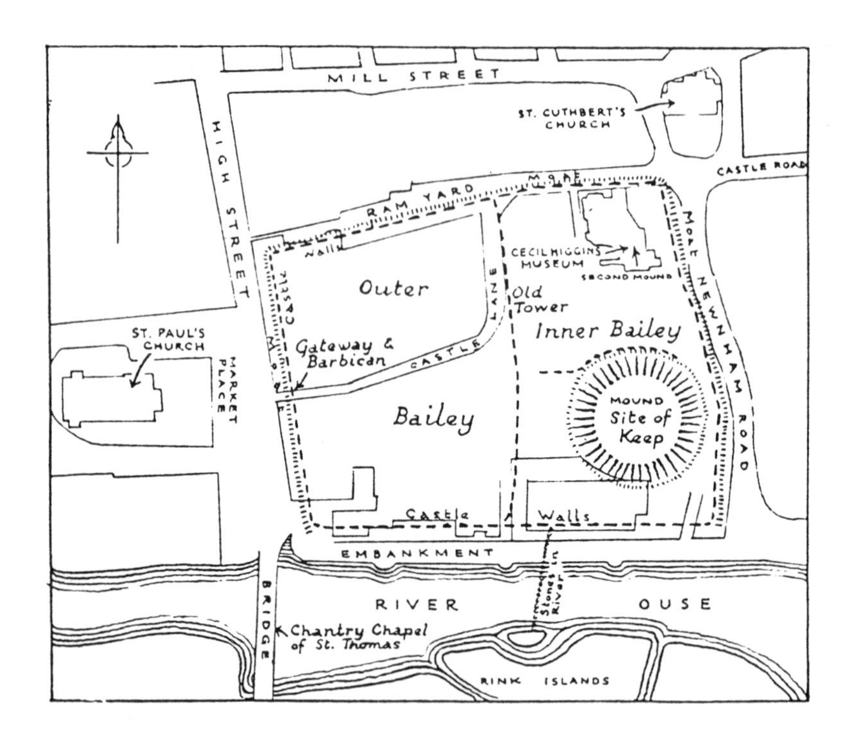

Bedford Castle – where it was and how it might have looked. The 'other' Fawkes was defeated here in 1224.

preparing to confront the king. Many of them marched down from the north and linked up with William de Beauchamp at Bedford Castle. The king sent Fawkes to subdue Bedford Castle, which he did successfully on December 2nd 1215. For this Fawkes was rewarded by being given the castle, which he proceeded to enlarge and fortify.

King John increasingly relied on Fawkes and left him in charge in London while he, the king, moved north to subdue the northern barons. That expedition proved ill-starred and King John died.

His son and heir to the throne was the nine-year old Henry. A Council of State was appointed to rule on behalf of the boy monarch. On that Council Fawkes served. In military terms his particular command covered all the castles in the midlands, from Oxford across to East Anglia.

In 1217 Fawkes relieved Lincoln Castle, taking William de Beauchamp prisoner in the process. In the same year Fawkes was made Sheriff of Bedfordshire. Thereafter the county became his power base. He already held Bedford Castle. In 1221 he acquired Luton and built a castle there too. To clear space for the building of that castle Fawkes was ruthless in evicting people from their lands. At least a hundred fifty people suffered in this way.

Fawkes not only took peoples' lands, he also deprived others of water, by his construction of his own dam. One result of this was that the mill in Luton, owned by St. Albans Abbey, could no longer grind.

The nine-year old Henry grew up. He was to have a long reign as Henry III, from 1216 to 1272. Fawkes continued to serve the young monarch and kept his place in the Council of State. In 1217 and again in 1225 he helped to confirm and implement the clauses of the Magna Carta secured at Runnemede in 1215. So the mercenary soldier born in France had done well in England and was a power in the land – particularly in his adopted county of Bedfordshire.

Perhaps he had become too powerful – too prone to take the law into his own hands. He seemed unable to realise that times had changed. His acts of violence increased. Once he murdered a monk from Warden Abbey. On other occasions he carried off other monks and imprisoned them in Bedford Castle. He continually quarrelled with the monks of St. Albans.

His wife grew alarmed at her husband's behaviour. Her anxiety was increased by a dream and she begged him to desist. To soothe her anxieties Fawkes agreed to mend his ways and even agreed to submit to discipline imposed by the Abbot of St. Albans.

In 1224 Judges arrived in Dunstable to look into Fawkes' behaviour. No less than thirty charges were brought against him. He was found guilty of all of them and was heavily fined. Even then Fawkes showed he had not learned his lesson – he seized one of the Judges, Henry de Braybrook, and carried him off in chains to Bedford Castle!

All this was too much for King Henry III. He decided it was time to bring Fawkes to heel. He was grateful for the service Fawkes had rendered him during his minority, but he decided he must now trim Fawkes down to size.

So the king came to Bedford in person to lay siege to Bedford Castle. He had summoned Sheriffs from elsewhere and he had collected a considerable force of soldiers, including many skilled in the art of attacking a fortified castle. The Siege of Bedford Castle began.

The outer walls were breached first by the stones hurled at them from the ballista; inner walls were then undermined. Two wooden towers were erected from which archers could fire into the castle. Soon the barbican entrance was breached and the men of Dunstable surged into the outer bailey. They set fire to the corn and hay stored there. The king's men came finally into the inner bailey and the assault on the central tower began.

The garrison of Bedford Castle was commanded by Fawkes' brother. When the central tower finally collapsed the garrison surrendered. Eighty were hanged. Fawkes himself was not taken but he surrendered himself to the king soon after. It might have been expected that he too would be hanged, but he wasn't. No doubt the good service he had rendered in earlier years saved him. He was exiled from the kingdom and died in France soon afterwards.

So died the other Fawkes. He has no day in our calendar to commemorate his exploits, as his later namesake has. Luton Castle is no more. Bedford Castle was ordered to be largely demolished. Some of its stones were recycled for building at Caldwell and Newnham Priories.

Fawkes had first acquired Bedford Castle as a reward for subduing it when it was owned and occupied by William de Beauchamp. Justice was now done to the extent that William was given back what was left of the castle. He was permitted to build a dwelling house there but was forbidden to crennelate it. He lived to a great age and, like the defeated and exiled Fawkes, he too became Sheriff of Bedfordshire.

Chapter 19

Sisters Under the Skin

In one of his poems, which he called 'The Ladies', Rudyard Kipling wrote:

'The Colonel's Lady an' Judy O'Grady
Are sisters under their skin.'

Here are four ladies from the pages of English history. All belong to our region, to Bedfordshire, Buckinghamshire and Hertfordshire. The earliest belongs to the 12th century, the second to the 16th, the third to the 17th, and the last to the 19th century. They couldn't be more diverse, and yet in a strange way they were 'sisters under the skin'. They are:

'The Lady of the Wood'
'The Nine Days Wonder'
'The Wicked Lady'
and
'The Jolly Barmaid'

The Lady of the Wood

A 12th century merchant in Huntingdon rejoiced at the birth of a daughter. The family were of good stock, descendents of minor Saxon aristocracy preceding the Conquest. The baby girl was christened Christina and grew to a beautiful young womanhood. She showed early signs of being a highly intelligent girl. If she had been born centuries later she would probably have achieved fame as, say, the Principal of a women's college at Oxford or Cambridge. Her parents were rightly proud of her and hoped she would make a good marriage.

When Christina was fourteen the whole family went to visit S.t Albans Abbey. That great building already had its fine Norman nave and the young Christina was much moved by it. After attending Mass there Christina made her own was back to the High Altar. Kneeling there she made a private vow to serve God.

In her later teens the question of a suitable marriage for her much occupied her parents' minds. A young man named Berhed wished to marry her and her parents approved. But Christina declined. For a whole year she maintained her refusal, to the great puzzlement of her parents. After sustained pressure Christina reluctantly agreed to be betrothed. But secretly she was determined not to be wed.

When there seemed to be no other way out, Christina decided to run away. With the help of a servant who procured a horse for her, and dressing herself in men's clothes, she made her escape. She went first to Flamstead and there sought the help of a recluse named Alwen. But that was only a temporary refuge for her. She travelled on from Flamstead towards Dunstable and came to the lodging of an old hermit named Roger.

Roger scarcely knew what to do with this strange runaway. He quickly sensed that she was no ordinary person and he accepted that she believed herself to be called by God. He made a cell for her where for four years she lived the life of an anchoress. In that time she matured; her determination to devote herself to God's service strengthened. Roger was much moved by her obvious piety. He called he 'myn sunendaege dohter' – 'my Sunday daughter'.

Meanwhile her parents had come to accept that for Christina the ordinary ways of family life had long ceased, and that marriage would play no part in her future. Berhed accepted this too, and in Roger's presence he formally released her from her betrothal. Later, Roger the old hermit died and Christina inherited his cell.

Christina's reputation and piety and wisdom increased year by year. Geoffrey, the Abbot of St. Albans, learned to rely on her counsel. Christina was asked to take charge of a community of nuns at York, but she declined. She hoped that it would be possible to found a Priory for Benedictine Nuns in Bedfordshire. This was finally agreed to, after consultations between the Dean and Chapter of St. Pauls and Abbot Geoffrey of St. Albans.

The Benedictine Priory was established at Markyate in the year 1145, with Christina as its first Prioress. Here her natural talents and her deep sense of vocation found their outlet. She was able to organise and to administer, and she could both live a life of conventual piety and teach others to do the same.

The English Pope

Prioress Christina had one other attribute – she was a skilled embroiderer. She embroidered beautiful mitres and sent them as gifts to Pope Adrian IV. Perhaps she was moved to do so because the Pope was an Englishman – the only Englishman ever to be Pope in the long history of the papacy. What is more, he was a Bedfordshire man, born in 1100 at Abbots Langley near St. Albans! His name was Nicholas Breakspear. He became Pope in 1154, nine years after Christina's Priory was established at Markyate.

There we leave Christina in her Benedictine Priory at Markyate. But before this chapter ends we shall return to Markyate, to consider another remarkable woman in that very place.

❖ ❖ ❖ ❖ ❖

A Nine Days' Wonder

In 1537 a daughter was born to Henry Grey, Marquess of Dorset. Her mother, Frances was the daughter of the Duke of Suffolk. The baby was baptised with the name of Jane and grew to be a beautiful girl. A clever girl too. She was tutored by John Aylmer, a future Bishop of London, and proved to be a talented linguist. In her teens, and much against her will, she was married to young Lord Guildford Dudley.

The king at the time of Jane's marriage was Edward VI. He

was a minor and therefore could only rule with a Lord Protector. That Lord Protector was John Dudley, the Earl of Warwick. Jane's young husband was the Lord Protector's son.

King Edward VI was not only a minor, he was also sickly and not expected to live long. When he died, who would succeed him? That question vexed the minds of many people. Ready to hand were two strong candidates for the throne – the two half-sisters of the young king. They were Mary, the daughter of Catherine of Aragon, whom Henry VIII had divorced, and Elizabeth, the daughter of Anne Boleyn, whom Henry VIII had executed.

But there were those in high places who wanted neither of these to be queen. Among these was the Lord Protector, the Earl of Warwick. That was why he had insisted on his son, Guildford Dudley, marrying the young Jane Grey. It was all part of his plot that when the sickly Edward VI died, the throne should go neither to Mary nor to Elizabeth, but to Jane Grey. As a granddaughter of Henry VII she was of royal Tudor descent and her accession to the throne would neatly by-pass the two half-sisters who were daughters of Henry VIII.

The powerful Grey family were naturally excited at the prospect. All of them, that is, except Jane Grey herself. She had no more desire to be queen than she had been to marry Guildford Dudley. A cousin of Jane Grey's father was Baron Grey of Water Hall, Bletchley. He was thrilled at the thought that a kinswoman of his would be queen. He made plans that as soon as Edward VI died, he would muster support for Jane to be proclaimed Queen in Aylesbury.

But things moved too fast for Baron Grey of Bletchley. For one thing his neighbour, Sir William Dormer of Wing, quickly staged his own proclamation naming Mary as Queen. More to the point, Mary herself ensured her own proclamation in London. And she left nothing to chance. She despatched her half-sister Elizabeth to virtual imprisonment at Woodstock. And she clapped both Jane Grey and her husband into the Tower where both of them were executed.

So, although the Lord Protector had proclaimed Jane Grey

as Queen the moment Edward VI died, her 'reign' lasted just nine days. Poor Jane's father, the Duke of Suffolk, joined in a short-lived abortive rebellion on Jane's behalf, led by Sir Thomas Wyatt. On 12th February 1554 Jane was beheaded with her husband.

The triumphant Mary I took her revenge on all who had wanted Jane to be queen. William, Lord Grey of Wilton and Bletchley, was arrested and imprisoned. He was later pardoned but was stripped of his honours and estates. It could have been worse. Mary I only reigned for five years. When she was succeeded by Elizabeth I, Lord Grey's honours and estates in Bletchley were restored to him in 1559. That was some consolation to him. But the young, beautiful and intelligent Jane Grey his kinswoman paid the price with her life - executed simply because she was a Tudor who might have kept Mary I from the throne.

❖❖❖❖❖

The Wicked Lady

We return again to Markyate. In the 12th century we considered the blessed Christina, a very holy lady and the first Prioress of Markyate Nunnery. Now we have come back to Markyate in the 17th century, and it is 'the Wicked Lady' we are now to consider.

In the interval much happened at Markyate. In the 16th century, in common with all religious houses, the Benedictine Priory at Markyate was closed down. The lands and buildings were disposed of and the new owners could do as they wished with the property they had now acquired.

Over the centuries what had begun as no more than a tiny hermit's cell had grown into a nunnery of modest size. By 1539 the main building was a house of some proportions. The first lay person to own Markyate was Humphrey Bourchier. He found that he had 'much cost in translating of the priory into a manor-place'.

By the middle of the 17th century the Manor at Markyate was owned by Sir Ralph Ferrers, who also had a London town house in Lincoln's Inn's Fields. He was unmarried. Nearby, between Markyate and Hemel Hempstead there lived a well-to-do landowner named John Worth. His lands bordered the Markyate estates. He had a teenage daughter, Catherine, born in 1662. John Worth was anxious that Catherine should marry Sir Ralph. As Lady Catherine Ferrers she would enjoy great status as the Lady of the Manor. And her fond father could imagine her becoming a great hostess in London society too.

There was one slight snag. The sixteen-year old Catherine did not want to be married to Sir Ralph. She was a high-spirited girl, very beautiful, with flame-coloured hair, bewitching green eyes, and a pale cream-coloured skin. She loved life and hoped for excitement and adventure. She saw no prospect of these married to Sir Ralph whom she considered dull and boring.

But parental pressure won the day. Catherine married Sir Ralph and became Lady Catherine Ferrers. Sadly, her life at Markyate was as boring as she had feared it would be. Her husband was a poor lover, more interested in his estate than in his young wife. No children were born to the union. Catherine felt bored and frustrated.

Then one day she heard people talking about a highwayman who had carried out a robbery on the nearby Watling Street. A mad idea seized hold of Catherine. To relieve her boredom why shouldn't she play at being a highwayman!

Heavily disguised in men's clothes she rode off into the night. (More than five hundred years before in that same countryside the young Christina, disguised as a man had ridden off into the night. Christina's flight had been to avoid marriage and to seek a way of serving God. Catherine's flight was to escape from a boring marriage and to seek adventure.)

Ironically, the first victim of the Lady-of-the-Manor-turned-Highwayman was the sister of the Lord of the Manor! Catherine hated her sister-in-law and was delighted to relieve her of her cash and her jewels. She was even more delighted as she heard her sister-in-law giving an indignant account of the robbery to her brother.

From then on from time to time Catherine slipped out of the house at night to pursue her new career. In the daytime she carried on as the dutiful Lady of the Manor. But one night she challenged a lone horseman who forced her to remove her mask. When he recovered from the shock of finding that she was a woman, the man declared himself to be a highwayman – Jerry Jackman by name. He suggested that from then on they should work as partners!

All went well with their partnership till the night of 10th June 1683. That night when the pair attempted one more robbery their victim put up such resistance that Catherine shot him!

Next day Sir Ralph Ferrers, still astonishingly unaware of his wife's double life, put up a reward of £50 for anyone able to name the highwayman responsible. A trusted servant at Markyate Manor who had discovered what Lady Catherine had been doing begged her to give up her nefarious night-time activities lest she brought shame to the family's good name. Catherine agreed. The old servant promised to keep her secret and was as good as his word. Within a year he had died, taking her secret with him to the grave.

Meanwhile Jerry Jackman had been caught, tried and hanged. On a summer's night in 1684 Lady Catherine succumbed to the temptation to have another go. It proved to be one adventure too many. She was herself shot and wounded and only with difficulty found her way back to Markyate Manor where she died on the stairs.

These astonishing exploits of Lady Catherine Ferrers have inspired one novel and two famous films. The novel was written in 1944 by Magdalen King-Hall. She called it 'The Life and Death of the Wicked Lady Skelton'.

In 1945 came the first film version, called 'The Wicked Lady'. Margaret Lockwood played the part of Catherine. A second version of the film was also made later.

The Wicked Lady's exploits have left a number of ghost stories behind. And one mystery – no one knows where Catherine is buried. Some say she lies in an unmarked grave in

Hitchin. There is a postscript too – when it was decided to rebuild Markyate Manor in 1840 no local people would undertake the task, fearing the ghosts. Contractors had to be brought in from London to do the work.

❖❖❖❖❖

The Jolly Barmaid

When the Bourbon royal family was forced into exile by the French Revolution they eventually sought asylum in Britain. The British Government not only financed their stay in this country, they also generously offered them a home in Holy Rood Palace in Edinburgh. But King Louis declined this offer because Scotland was too far away and he wanted to be in or near London.

After a brief stay at Stowe the French Court in Exile settled at Hartwell House, two miles outside Aylesbury. Altogether the French colony amounted to some one hundred and fifty persons. The exile lasted many years and was only finally brought to an end when Napoleon was defeated at Waterloo in 1815. Then Louis could return to France and claim his throne.

The exile was a very sad and uncertain time for the French at Hartwell, made all the sadder by the death there of the king's wife. Through it all King Louis earned the reputation of being a quiet, wise and dignified man. He was dubbed 'The Sage of Hartwell'.

From time to time during his exile the king and his ministers had occasion to go up to London. Each time they did so they would change horses at The Kings Arms Inn at Berkhamsted. Mine Host at The Kings Arms was of course delighted at this patronage by foreign royalty. He had several daughters. The eldest daughter was a jolly, outgoing sort of young lady. She loved the excitement of the comings and goings of King Louis and his entourage. She always made a point of being on hand to welcome the king and to chat with him while the horses were being changed.

The day the news came that Napoleon had been defeated the king at once travelled to London. As always, the Landlord's daughter was there to greet him at Berkhamsted. She congratulated His Majesty of this change in his fortunes but she realised that soon the king and his party would come no more to change their horses at The Kings Arms.

The king thanked her for her congratulations and said that when he was once more in his palace in France she must come to visit him there. So in due course there came the day when the jolly barmaid did indeed go to Paris to visit the king. She was made welcome and given accommodation in the Tuileries.

She asked the king – would he not feel more comfortable back in the peace and tranquility at Hartwell, instead of in all the tiresome formality of the French Court in Paris? The king replied: 'Madam, I have always felt it my duty to make myself comfortable in every situation to which I am called'.

Of course there were prudes and mischief-makers who made snide remarks about this relationship between the King of France and an English barmaid. On her return home the barmaid heard of these remarks. So, being the bright and cheerful person she was, accustomed always to speaking her mind, she wrote a letter to the Hertford Newspaper, pouring scorn on these false accusations, and roundly asserting that 'the only King's Arms I was ever in were The Kings Arms at Berkhamsted'.

❖❖❖❖❖

Our quartet of ladies is now complete – the beautiful but pious Christina, of the 13th century Priory of Saint-Trinity-in-the-Wood at Markyate; the beautiful but tragic Lady Jane Grey in the 16th century, beheaded in the Tower of London; the beautiful but Wicked Lady of the Manor of Markyate in the 17th century; and the extrovert barmaid of The Kings Arms in Berkhamsted in the 19th century.

The four are so varied both in their dates and in the events in which they shared. Yet, like 'The Colonel's Lady and Judy O'Grady', they really are all 'sisters under the skin'. All four were larger than life characters; each in her own way created her own niche in English History.

Chapter 20

As a Matter of Fact

Rudolph Diesel was a German engineer but he was born in Paris in 1858. His early interest was refrigeration but in 1885 he turned his attention to internal combustion engines. The great Krupps firm subsidised him. He was seeking what he called 'a rational heat motor', and in 1897 he demonstrated his first practical compression-ignited engine. The Diesel engine achieved an efficiency twice that of comparable steam engines. In 1913 Rudolph Diesel vanished from the Antwerp-Harwich Mail Steamer and was presumed drowned. So he has no known grave, but his name survives the world over in diesel fuel.

BUT AS A MATTER OF FACT we can look much nearer home for the true ancestor of modern oil engines. Between 1886 and 1890, at Bletchley Ironworks in Denmark Street Herbert Akroyd Stuart devised an oil engine which injected 'solid fuel' – in other words oil without air – to drive a piston. He made at least eight such engines in his Bletchley Foundry and then sold the patent in 1892 to Hornby and Sons of Grantham. Thereafter thousands of 'Hornby-Akroyd' engines were made and went into use all over the world.

Bletchley Ironworks has long since disappeared, but today a plaque on the wall at the corner of Denmark Street in Bletchley records the fact that:

On this site Herbert Akroyd Stuart
(1864–1927)
Evolved the first operational
heavy-oil engine Patented 1890.

❖ ❖ ❖ ❖ ❖

Mursley near Bletchley is a village, picturesque but small. Yet in the Middle Ages it was a small market town. The village church contains several monuments to the Fortescues. A mile away across the fields stand two modest farm houses. Altogether, a truly rural scene. BUT AS A MATTER OF FACT those farm houses stand were in 1590 Sir John Fortescue built one of the finest country houses in all England. It was called Salden House and it was lavish. It cost £33,000 to build, an astronomical sum in today's money.

Sir John Fortescue was a second cousin once removed of Queen Elizabeth. He was a man of great learning and was selected to superintend the studies of the young Elizabeth. She went on to become Queen in 1558, and in 1589 she appointed Sir John as Chancellor of the Exchequer. He became a very wealthy man and applied much of his wealth to the building of his magnificent Salden House. There, on several occasions, he entertained Queen Elizabeth, and her successor James I.

Sir John represented Buckinghamshire in Parliament for several years. He was the friend of all the leading figures of the day – Burleigh, Bacon, Raleigh, Essex.

Son succeeded to son at Salden House near Mursley until 1729 when the Fortescue title became extinct. It was not only the title which then expired – so too had the family wealth. The great house had by then lost most of its former glory. In 1730 it was demolished and no trace of it now remains.

But in Fenny Stratford there is a memento of the once great Salden House. When the House was being demolished Browne Willis, Lord of the Manors of Bletchley and Fenny Stratford, for thirty shillings, bought a job-lot of stain glass. He used some of this to adorn his own house, Water Hall. The rest he had fashioned into a window for St. Martin's Church which he was then building in Fenny Stratford. At the bottom right hand corner of the window are the Arms of Anne Boleyn, the mother of Queen Elizabeth.

Charles I.

It goes without saying that the Civil War in the 17th century profoundly affected every part of England. There were many battles and even more minor skirmishes. Most counties experienced none of these on their own soil but all of them were affected by them.

AS A MATTER OF FACT it fell to the County of Northamptonshire to record the very first blood shed in the Civil War. It happened at Kilsby even before the war itself technically began.

It was in 1642 that King Charles raised his Standard at Nottingham, marking the outbreak of hostilities. But two weeks before he did so, a small troop of Cavaliers rode into the village

The Civil War began when Charles raised his Standard in 1642 at Nottingham. But the first blood had already been spilt two weeks before in Northamptonshire.

Warrant to Execute King Charles the First. AD 1648.

At the high Court of Justice for the tryinge and judginge of Charles Steuart Kinge of England January xxixth Anno Dni 1648.

Whereas Charles Steuart Kinge of England is and standeth convicted attaynted and condemned of High Treason and other high Crymes And sentence uppon Saturday last was pronounced against him by this Court to be putt to death by the severinge of his head from his body Of wch sentence execucon yet remayneth to be done These are therefore to will and require you to see the said sentence executed In the open Streete before Whitehall uppon the morrowe being the Thirtieth day of this instante moneth of January betweene the houres of Tenn in the morninge and Five in the afternoone of the same day wth full effect And for soe doing this shall be yor sufficient warrant And these are to require All Officers and Souldiers and other the good people of this Nation of England to be assistinge unto you in this service Given under our hands and Seales.

To Collonell ffrancis Hacker Collonell Huncks and Lieutenant Collonell Phayre and to every of them

Jo: Bradshawe · Tho: Grey · O. Cromwell · Edw. Whalley · M. Livesey · John Okey · J. Danvers · Jo: Bourchier · H. Ireton · Tho. Mauleverer · Har: Waller · John Blakiston · J. Hutchinson · Willi. Goffe · Tho. Pride · Pe. Temple · T. Harrison · J. Hewson · Hen. Smyth · Per. Pelham · Ri. Deane · Robert Tichborne · H. Edwardes · Daniel Blagrave · Owen Rowe · William Purefoy · Ad. Scrope · James Temple · A. Garland · Edm. Ludlowe · Henry Marten · Vinct. Potter · Wm. Constable · Rich. Ingoldesby · Will. Cawley · Jo. Barkstead · Isaa. Ewer · John Dixwell · Valentine Wauton · Symon Mayne · Tho. Horton · J. Jones · John Moore · Gilbt. Millington · G. Fleetwood · J. Alured · Robt. Lilburne · Will. Say · Anth. Stapley · Gre. Norton · Tho. Challoner · Tho. Wogan · John Venn · Gregory Clement · Jo. Downes · Tho. Wayte · Tho. Scot · Jo. Carew · Miles Corbet

The Death Warrant of Charles I. Nine of the 26 regicides came from Buckinghamshire.

of Kilsby and killed some of the inhabitants.

That was the first blood to be shed in the Civil War. And to Northamptonshire also belongs the final battle of that war. It happened at Naseby, only ten miles from Kilsby. Though it is true that further fighting took place after the Battle of Naseby in 1645, effectively Cromwell's victory at Naseby marked the end of Royalist hopes. In the following year, 1646, King Charles surrendered.

❖ ❖ ❖ ❖ ❖

Not until 1746 did Sir John Fielding found the Bow Street Runners. And not until 1830 did Sir Robert Peel found the modern Police Force. (We still call them 'Bobbies' after Sir Robert.)

Before either of these innovations, in the 17th century the Militia were introduced, county by county. In each county the Lord-Lieutenant organised a Militia Levy. The obligation to provide men and arms was placed on property owners. Training was sometimes sketchy, but the Militia was the only force available to help keep law and order in the county.

A good example of the function of the Militia is seen in the part they played in Buckinghamshire in tackling the widespread outbreaks of violence in 1830 caused by the Machine Breakers inspired and led by the so-called 'Captain Swing'.

BUT AS A MATTER OF FACT, the Militia could sometimes be called on to serve far outside their own county borders. The Hertfordshire Militia were dramatically involved in 1793 as far away as Bristol. The London Times of 2nd October 1793 carried the story. It had to do with the immense unpopularity of Toll Gates. The Times reported:

TOLL GATE RIOTS

Bristol, Sept. 30.'

Last week a large mob assembled in consequence of the Toll being continued another year unexpectedly on the bridge and cut the toll gates to pieces, and turned the toll-keepers forcibly out. Other gates were immediately created on Saturday last, when about eight oclock in the evening, several thousand people assembled, set fire to the gates, and vowed vengeance to every opposer. The Mayor, several of the Corporation and all the constables attended and the Riot Act was read. The fire bells rang from several churches, but nothing would appease the tumult. Lord Bateman, at the head of the Hertfordshire Militia, were then called in, the drums beat to arms; they formed their lines, and were obliged to fire, for many people had been greatly hurt, and two of the Corporation had their heads broke, and the Mayor lost both hat and wig, and narrowly escaped being wounded.'

Continuing the story, The Times published the following: *Council-house, Bristol, Sept. 19th 1793. 'Whereas great numbers of persons did last night and this day assemble themselves together near Bristol-bridge, to the disturbance of the public peace, and have committed a capital felony, and other enormities, and the Proclamation directed by the Riot Act having at three oclock this afternoon been read, the Magistrates hereby give notice to all the peaceable inhabitants of this city not to appear in the streets or public places after the hour of six this afternoon, as the military who are now in readiness to assist the Civil Power will have orders to fire on such of the riotous persons who shall have remained together, after one hour from the time of the reading the said Proclamation.'*

❖❖❖❖❖

Eleven years after the Armistice, World War I claimed an unexpected and belated fatal casualty. In 1920 Aylesbury was presented with an Army Tank. For nine years it stood in Kingsbury Square.

In 1929 Aylesbury Town Council decided to have it removed. Orders were given for the tank to be cut up and taken away. A workman, using an acetylene torch, cut into the tank's petrol tank. Even after all these years, this still contained traces of the fuel. The tank exploded, killing the workman, and scattering bits of metal far and wide.

Chapter 21

Back to the Future

The future belongs to posterity - to the generations not yet born. The past belongs to our ancestors - the generations that have passed. And we are sitting in between - we are the present, neither future nor past.

In the 18th century Edmund Burke, a great philosophical and political thinker, once said:

> *'People will not look forward to posterity*
> *Who never look back to their ancestors.'*

In his own way Burke was making the point that if we wish to prepare for the future we must first learn from our past. 'Back to the future', then, is a sound principle, and not just a contradiction in terms.

There are countless ways of assessing the health of a society. One of them is to study the law courts - to examine what brings individuals into conflict with authority. They need not be only the High Courts, and the individuals on trial need not only be people of prominence. Petty Sessions will do very well, and what transpires there can be very instructive.

So let us take a look at the *Buckinghamshire Sessions Records* for the Midsummer Session at Buckingham in the reign of Charles II. The year is 1678.

Many of the cases before the Court that year sound very familiar to us. They are the sort of cases that can and do figure in Petty Sessions in our own day:

18 July 1678. Samuel Smith of London for cheating Thomas Fastnedge and John Prince out of £5 each.
Nathaniel Withers of Wendover for assaulting Mary Clark – fined 6s.8d.
Philip Gunne and Nathaniel Gune (sic) both of Bradwell for assaulting William Abbott.
William Welch. constable of Aylesbury, for neglect of duty.
Nicholas Bazill of Brill, James Osburne, John Bayly and John Drapier, all of Great Marlow, for keeping unlicensed alehouses.
Richard Jeffery of Tingewick for 'a dangerous chimney'.

The Old Gaol, Buckingham.

These cases, all dealt with on that one day, at Petty Sessions by our ancestors over 320 years ago, could be paralleled today. And, it may be, they will be matched again by our posterity in another 320 years time. But there were other cases in the Bucks. Sessions Records of 1678 which read very strangely today:

'Mary, wife of Toby Bowyer, Joseph Fryer, John Bovingdon, yeoman, Robert Coleman, Philip Harvey and Richard Langley, all of Great Marlow; Elizabeth West and Elizabeth Toovey, both of Turfield with Ipstone, and Elizabeth Keane of Fingest, all indicted for RECUSANCY.'

Brewer's Dictionary of Phrase & Fable explains Recusancy as 'the name given from the reign of Elizabeth I to those who refused to attend the services of the Church of England, (Latin "recusare", to refuse). The term commonly denoted 'popish recusants', although properly it also included protestant dissenters. Fines were first enacted under statute in 1552 and 1559 at the rate of 1s per Sunday, but raised to the exorbitant sum of £20 per month in 1587'.

The Bucks. Sessions Records of 1678–1681 show that the practice of fining recusants was still being briskly followed. On 16th January 1678 no fewer than sixty-one individuals were indicted for 'popish recusancy'. And again on 1st May 1679 another batch of twenty were similarly indicted. In July of that same year:

Mary Farmer of Great Marlow, spinster, who was committed to gaol as a popish recusant at the last Session for refusing to take the oaths of supremacy and allegiance, is ordered to be released on bail with two sureties of £40 each, on condition that she shall make her personall appearance before her Majesties Justices of his Court of King's Bench att Westminster on the first day of the Terme of St. Michell next ensueinge.'

Occasionally a much small number of protestant recusants appear in the Records, indicted for attending 'a protestant conventicle'. For example, the following is recorded:

May 1st 1678. 'Divers goods and chattells were distrained of several persons in this County for being legally convicted of beinge att Unlawful Conventicles. The Constables are ordered to sell the goods and to hand over the proceeds to certain justices.'

Similarly, on 22nd April 1680: *'Alexander Dover and John White, Petty Constable of Aylesbury, paid into court the sum of £2 10s 6d which had been levied upon certain persons convicted of beinge att a Conventicle.'*

Elsewhere in the Records we read of other individuals found guilty of 'not attending church'. And one individual, John Sloppe of Fenny Stratford, was found guilty of 'selling drink on Sunday during Divine Service'.

Viewed from the late 1990s, the notion obtaining in the 1680s that religious practice can be rigorously enforced by magistrates seems outlandish. Even less plausible is the notion that the Church of England has, and must have, a total monopoly of conformity. Projecting from the present to posterity, how will such matters be viewed three centuries from now?

Legislation in the 1990s is aimed at controlling certain breeds of dogs. The 1670s had its own unexpected precendent. Thus: 10th October 1678 *'George Cowley and John Sandwell, both of Buckingham indicted for keeping greyhounds contrary to the Statute'.*

Oddly enough, Magistrates in 1994 also had to deal with a case involving greyhounds, and Buckinghamshire figured in the affair. Two men from Wales had travelled to Bucks. with their greyhounds to meet a man from Liverpool.The intention was to demonstrate their greyhounds' hare-coursing prowess to the Liverpudlian. But he left the Welshmen stranded in the Buckinghamshire field with their greyhounds and drove off. The Welshmen, unemployed, with no money and no map, were in a quandary. In despair, they set off walking on the hard shoulder of the M4, with their greyhounds, Bella and Blackie, on leads. They figured that if they kept going, the M4 must eventually lead them to Wales. They were within twelve miles of the Severn Bridge when they finally sat down on the hard shoulder of the M4 with Bella and Blackie. All four, men and greyhounds, were by now utterly exhausted. There the Police found them. Magistrates at Chippenham Court fined both men

£65 each, with £25 costs. So the old saying about 'going to see a man about a dog' had an expensive ending for the Welshmen.

The problem confronting us in the 1990s of how to finance the maintenance of highways was a very familiar one in the reign of Charles II too. A constant battle was waged to make villages and towns pay for the roads in their own areas. Thus, on 18th July 1678, *'the inhabitants of Clifton Reynes are fined for not repairing a highway called Kit Close Land'.*

The village of Stewkley was in the same trouble on 10th October 1678, but at a later session they were discharged 'upon their bringing a certificate to show that their highway had been repaired'.

A major dispute about highway maintenance costs was settled on 17th July 1679:

'. . . agreement entered into between the inhabitants of Great Brickhill and the inhabitants of Little Brickhill concerning the liability to repair that part of the high road to London which lies between Little Brickhill and Mile House.'

Sixteen representatives signed on behalf of Great Brickhill, including John Duncombe, Lord of the Manor. Fourteen signed on behalf of Little Brickhill.

❖ ❖ ❖ ❖ ❖

Dealing with rogues, vagabonds and beggars was a major preoccupation in the late 17th century. In general the principle was that the cost of dealing with such characters must be born locally. The obvious solution was to send such people packing to where they came from as smartly as possible. The Sessions Records give many examples of this. And if strong arm tactics were needed, they were used.

Punishment could be, and frequently was, very severe, not to say brutal. Take this example:

'10th October 1679. 'Kelham Hebbes, convicted of stealing a bushel of wheat, value 10d., and William Bates, convicted of stealing a petticoat, value 6d., are ordered to be "made fast to the breech of a cart and stript naked from the wast upward, the proximate fryday, about one of the clock in the afternoon, and whipt from the Mercatt house in Chesham to the Great Elme att the upper end of the street, and soe

downe to the Mercatt house againe, untill their bodys be bloody".'

Similarly on 15th January 1680 Thomas Walton who had pleaded guilty to stealing 'one female asse, value 11d' was ordered to be 'whipped at the post untill his body be bloody'. The punishment doesn't seem to have reformed Thomas Walton, because on April 22nd 1680 he was again in court. This time he pleaded guilty to stealing a sheep, value 11d. This time the Court ordered that he 'be whipped at the tail of a cart from the Goale door to the George signe post in Aylesbury and down again to the goale doore untill his body be bloody'. (Interesting to notice that the spellings of goal and gaol gave trouble in the 17th century too!)

Whipping the wicked 'till the back be bloody' was standard practice from Tudor times. So the Bucks. Sessions in the 1660s had plenty of precedents to follow.

❖ ❖ ❖ ❖ ❖

Cripples (often spelt creeples) figure quite often in the Sessions Records. Clearly they were given short shrift. An entry on 16th January 1680 says: *'Upon the appeal of Fullmer concerning the Removeall of creeples it is ordered that all cripples comeinge or goinge Westward and brought to Denham shall be from there removed the direct way to Chalfont St. Peters and thus to their places of settlement'*. In other words, send them packing as fast as possible to where they came from.

Poaching and illegal fishing occurred in Charles II's days, as they still do today, and as they doubtless still will in centuries to come. And there is one other constantly recurring subject in the Sessions Records of 1678 to 1681 which still has its counterpart today. There was scarcely a single session then without its 'Bastardy Order'. It seems not improbable that this subject, familiar in the time of Charles II, and familiar to us too three centuries later, will also be familiar to posterity three centuries hence!

Chapter 22

When Love Came to Chicksands

Chicksands Priory in Bedfordshire was founded in 1150 by Countess Rose. It was a Priory for Nuns of the Gilbertine Order, the only House of that Order anywhere in England. It lasted for nearly four hundred years, but in the 1540s, in common with all Abbeys, Monasteries and Priories, it was closed down. Its revenues enriched the crown or were diverted to other projects. Its buildings and lands were disposed of and a succession of new owners made of Chicksands Priory what they wished.

In 1578 Chicksands passed to Richard Osborn, a London Grocer. By the time of the Civil War it had become the home of his descendant, Sir Peter Osborne.

Sir Peter was a stalwart Royalist, active on behalf of his king. He was no stay-at-home. His service to the royal cause took him as far as the Channel Islands where he held the Castle on Guernsey for the King. Such loyalty and service cost him dear. When the war ended in the defeat of the King Sir Peter was broken both in heart and fortune. But it might have been worse. His wife, Lady Osborne, had relatives on the Parliamentary side, and this fact secured that Sir Peter was able to recover Chicksands, though his lands were much reduced.

Lady Osborne bore her husband twelve children, seven sons and five daughters. Not all survived. Only three sons were alive when the Civil War ended and only one of these, Henry, lived at Chicksands.

Of the daughters, some were married and lived elsewhere. Only Dorothy lived at Chicksands. She was not yet married. At twenty-five she was bright and vivacious. Yet she found life at Chicksands lonely and empty. Her father had become much of a recluse after the war ended and seldom left his room. Her brother was often away from home on business.

So Dorothy was much alone with her memories of the past. And one of those memories was vivid still. It was the memory of the day, four years before, when she had saved her brother's life. It happened on the Isle of Wight. Dorothy and her brother were awaiting ship there to take them to France. Their father, Sir Peter, had retired to St. Malo after leaving Guernsey.

In an idle moment at the Inn, Dorothy's brother used his diamond ring to indulge in a little graffiti. With the diamond he scratched on the window pane a ribald gibe at Colonel Hammond, the Parliamentary Governor of the Isle of Wight. This was foolish in the extreme. To show Royalist sympathies was dangerous; and to insult the Parliamentary Governor in the process further compounded the offence.

When the ribald inscription was discovered a number of people were arrested, Dorothy and her brother among them. They were hailed before the Governor. It soon became clear to Dorothy that her brother would be found guilty and would pay dearly. So she announced to Colonel Hammond that she was the guilty party. This bogus confession saved her brother. Fortunately for her, Colonel Hammond was impressed by her beauty and he was sufficient of a gallant to treat her supposed naughtiness lightly. He contented himself with a reprimand. Dorothy and the others were all released.

That was four years ago. But it had repercussions. An observer of that incident four years before had been a young man named William Temple, freshly down from Cambridge, and about to set out on a tour of the Continent.

William was bowled over by Dorothy's beauty, and full of admiration for her courage in shielding her brother. Dorothy, for her part, was vastly taken by the young man. So romance was in the air.

But the path of true love was not likely to be smooth. Two huge impediments existed. To begin with, Dorothy's father was a prominent Royalist, and one of her brothers had died fighting for the King. William Temple's father, on the other hand, was Sir John Temple, who was a leading Cromwell supporter and had sat in the Long Parliament. He held high office in Ireland and had ambitious plans for his son's future marriage and career.

The second impediment was financial. In the reduced circumstances in which the Osbornes found themselves, there was little prospect of an adequate dowry for Dorothy to take into a marriage. Custom decreed in those days that marriages were arranged and negotiated – they were seldom left to young lovers to settle for themselves.

So the young couple could only wait and hope. They pledged their love to each other and kept their strange courtship secret. They seldom met. Dorothy was alone at Chicksands, where her father still kept to his room. William Temple was in London where he was expected to embark on a diplomatic career. Only letter-writing was left to keep the young lovers in touch, and this could only be conducted in secret.

They wrote to each other faithfully every week and, though William's letters to Dorothy have not survived, her letters to him exist to this day, three centuries later.

From Chicksands to London is only about forty miles. There was, of course, no postal service in the 17th century. But every day carriers drove their waggons full of produce, plus a few passengers, from Bedfordshire into the capital. To these carriers Dorothy entrusted her letters to William. They were variously addressed – to tradesmen or lodging-house keepers in London – and from them William would collect them, with a tip or fee to the supposed addressees.

So time passed and the would-be lovers kept in touch. There were others who would have married Dorothy if they could. Ironically one of these was Henry Cromwell, the second son of the great Oliver Cromwell himself.

It amused Dorothy in her letters to William to tell him of these other would-be suitors. She shared with him, too, lots of gossip and jokes, and news of her travels whenever she left Chicksands. But the day when they might at last be joined in marriage seemed as remote as ever.

At last, however, Dorothy's father, Sir Peter Osborne, died. Much now depended on her brother Henry. He had always objected to William Temple, but now he came round and was prepared to sanction Dorothy's marriage to William. The necessary negotiations were completed and Dorothy prepared to leave Chicksands for ever.

She travelled in great excitement to London with Lady Peyton to buy her trousseau. William had already given her his ring. Dorothy and Lady Peyton lodged at first in Drury Lane, but hastily changed their lodging when they discovered someone there with smallpox. Alas, Dorothy soon felt unwell herself and, on November 9th, she too came down with smallpox.

Unlike so many, she recovered. But, also like so many, she found that her beauty had gone and the dreaded pock marks disfigured her. But the faithful William had not loved her all these seven years just for her looks alone.

So, on Christmas Day, 1654, Dorothy and William were wed. William went on to a successful diplomatic career with Dorothy at his side. She bore him seven children. So on this happy note our true Chicksands love story ends.

INDEX

Books Published by THE BOOK CASTLE

JOURNEYS INTO HERTFORDSHIRE: Anthony Mackay.
Foreword by The Marquess of Salisbury, Hatfield House. Nearly 200 superbly detailed ink drawings depict the towns, buildings and landscape of this still predominantly rural county.

JOURNEYS INTO BEDFORDSHIRE: Anthony Mackay.
Foreword by The Marquess of Tavistock, Woburn Abbey.
A lavish book of over 150 evocative ink drawings.

COUNTRYSIDE CYCLING IN BEDFORDSHIRE, BUCKINGHAMSHIRE AND HERTFORDSHIRE: Mick Payne.
Twenty rides on and off-road for all the family.

LEAFING THROUGH LITERATURE: Writers' Lives in Hertfordshire and Bedfordshire: David Carroll.
Illustrated short biographies of many famous authors and their connections with these counties.

THROUGH VISITORS' EYES: A Bedfordshire Anthology:
edited by Simon Houfe.
Impressions of the county by famous visitors over the last four centuries, thematically arranged and illustrated with line drawings.

THE HILL OF THE MARTYR: An Architectural History of St. Albans Abbey: Eileen Roberts.
Scholarly and readable chronological narrative history of Hertfordshire and Bedfordshire's famous cathedral. Fully illustrated with photographs and plans.

LOCAL WALKS: South Bedfordshire and North Chilterns:
Vaughan Basham. Twenty-seven thematic circular walks.

LOCAL WALKS: North and Mid-Bedfordshire:
Vaughan Basham. Twenty-five thematic circular walks.

CHILTERN WALKS: Hertfordshire, Bedfordshire and North Buckinghamshire: Nick Moon.
Part of the trilogy of circular walks, in association with the Chiltern Society. Each volume contains thirty circular walks.

CHILTERN WALKS: Buckinghamshire: Nick Moon.

CHILTERN WALKS: Oxfordshire and West Buckinghamshire:
Nick Moon.

OXFORDSHIRE WALKS: Oxford, the Cotswolds and the Cherwell Valley: Nick Moon.
One of two volumes planned to complement Chiltern Walks: Oxfordshire and complete coverage of the county, in association with the Oxford Fieldpaths Society. Thirty circular walks in each.

OXFORDSHIRE WALKS: Oxford, the Downs and the Thames Valley: Nick Moon.

FOLK: Characters and Events in the History of Bedfordshire and Northamptonshire: Vivienne Evans.
Anthology about people of yesteryear – arranged alphabetically by village or town.

LEGACIES: Tales and Legends of Luton and the North Chilterns: Vic Lea. Twenty-five mysteries and stories based on fact, including Luton Town Football Club. Many photographs.

ECHOES: Tales And Legends of Bedfordshire and Hertfordshire: Vic Lea. Thirty, compulsively retold historical incidents.

ECCENTRICS and VILLAINS, HAUNTINGS and HEROES. Tales from Four Shires: Northants., Beds., Bucks. and Herts.: John Houghton.
True incidents and curious events covering one thousand years.

THE RAILWAY AGE IN BEDFORDSHIRE: Fred Cockman.
Classic, illustrated account of early railway history.

JOHN BUNYAN: HIS LIFE AND TIMES: Vivienne Evans.
Foreword by the Bishop of Bedford. Preface by Terry Waite. Bedfordshire's most famous son set in his seventeenth century context.

SWANS IN MY KITCHEN: The Story of a Swan Sanctuary: Lis Dorer. Foreword by Dr Philip Burton. Updated edition. Tales of her dedication to the survival of these beautiful birds through her sanctuary near Hemel Hempstead.

WHIPSNADE WILD ANIMAL PARK: 'MY AFRICA': Lucy Pendar.
Foreword by Andrew Forbes. Introduction by Gerald Durrell.
Inside story of sixty years of the Park's animals and people – full of anecdotes, photographs and drawings.

FARM OF MY CHILDHOOD, 1925–1947: Mary Roberts.
An almost vanished lifestyle on a remote farm near Flitwick.

DUNSTABLE WITH THE PRIORY, 1100–1550: Vivienne Evans.
Dramatic growth of Henry I's important new town around a major crossroads.

DUNSTABLE DECADE: THE EIGHTIES: – A Collection of Photographs: Pat Lovering.
A souvenir book of nearly 300 pictures of people and events in the 1980s.

DUNSTABLE IN DETAIL: Nigel Benson.
A hundred of the town's buildings and features, plus town trail map.

OLD DUNSTABLE: Bill Twaddle.
A new edition of this collection of early photographs.

BOURNE AND BRED: A Dunstable Boyhood Between the Wars: Colin Bourne. An elegantly written, well-illustrated book capturing the spirit of the town over fifty years ago.

ROYAL HOUGHTON: Pat Lovering.
Illustrated history of Houghton Regis from the earliest times to the present.

BEDFORDSHIRE'S YESTERYEARS Vol. 1: The Family, Childhood and Schooldays: Brenda Fraser-Newstead.
Unusual early 20th century reminiscences, with private photographs.

BEDFORDSHIRE'S YESTERYEARS Vol 2: The Rural Scene: Brenda Fraser-Newstead.
Vivid first-hand accounts of country life two or three generations ago.

THE CHANGING FACE OF LUTON: An Illustrated History: Stephen Bunker, Robin Holgate and Marian Nichols.
Luton's development from earliest times to the present busy industrial town. Illustrated in colour and monochrome. The three authors from Luton Museum are all experts in local history, archaeology, crafts and social history.

THE MEN WHO WORE STRAW HELMETS: Policing Luton, 1840–1974: Tom Madigan.
Meticulously chronicled history; dozens of rare photographs; author served Luton Police for nearly fifty years.

BETWEEN THE HILLS: The Story of Lilley, a Chiltern Village: Roy Pinnock.
A priceless piece of our heritage – the rural beauty remains but the customs and way of life described here have largely disappeared.

EVA'S STORY: Chesham Since the Turn of the Century: Eva Rance.
The ever-changing twentieth-century, especially the early years at her parents' general stores, Tebby's, in the High Street.

THE TALL HITCHIN SERGEANT: A Victorian Crime Novel based on fact: Edgar Newman. Mixes real police officers and authentic background with an exciting storyline.

Specially for Children

VILLA BELOW THE KNOLLS: A Story of Roman Britain: Michael Dundrow. An exciting adventure for young John in Totternhoe and Dunstable two thousand years ago.

ADVENTURE ON THE KNOLLS: A Story of Iron Age Britain: Michael Dundrow. Excitement on Totternhoe Knolls as ten-year-old John finds himself back in those dangerous times, confronting Julius Caesar and his army.

THE RAVENS: One Boy Against the Might of Rome: James Dyer.
On the Barton Hills and in the south-each of England as the men of the great fort of Ravensburgh (near Hexton) confront the invaders.

Further titles are in preparation.
All the above are available via any bookshop, or from the publisher and bookseller

THE BOOK CASTLE
12 Church Street, Dunstable, Bedfordshire, LU5 4RU
Tel: (0582) 605670

ABOUT OXFAM

In 1942, a group of people met in Oxford to express their concern at the plight of Greek women and children, who were starving because of Nazi occupation and an Allied blockade of Greece. They asked the British Government to allow food supplies through to the innocent victims and permission for this was granted one year later. Meanwhile, funds were raised and life-saving supplies were sent to Greece via the Red Cross.

The group called themselves the Oxford Committee for Famine Relief and OXFAM became the telegram address.

Today, more than fifty years later, Oxfam is working in over 70 countries throughout the world, giving support to poor people irrespective of race, colour, gender, politics or religion.

Oxfam's work overseas is managed by teams of international and national staff operating from some 40 centres. They oversee programmes of emergency relief and development assistance and supply information to those making decisions that affect poor people.

Natural disasters and conflict continue to affect poor people in vulnerable communities. When emergencies occur, Oxfam responds quickly, working with local staff to assess the situation in order to respond in the most appropriate way. Oxfam staff co-ordinate their own work with local government officials and other organisations to provide shelter, water supplies and sanitation, medical care, and food. Thousands of refugees and people displaced by conflict are supported by Oxfam every year.

Oxfam has been at the forefront of moves to tighten international law on landmines, which threaten people in many countries where the organisation works.

Oxfam helps many communities throughout the world to survive disaster, to prevent disaster, and to restart community life once disaster has passed.

The organisation's well-renowned expertise in health and water is called on round the world, by other agencies and governments too.

Meeting community needs: Oxfam helps many poor communities who have never had decent health care, education or water supplies, or who have seen drastic cuts imposed on already meagre services. Oxfam offers advice, encouragement and direct support for people's own initiatives. Often, communities are helped in several ways at the same time – for example, improving water supplies, developing health care and expanding agriculture – so that everyone in the community will benefit.

Making a living: Oxfam supports poor people's efforts to become self-sufficient and to build a more secure life. Often, the sort of help Oxfam gives in these cases is far removed from traditional ideas of aid: training, help for simple credit schemes, and backing for groups trying to pool their resources – all things which can be shared and repeated with a minimum amount of outside help.

Defending rights: Many people are poor, powerless or insecure because their rights are denied. Oxfam works with people struggling to hold onto their land and culture, and organisations which are making people aware of their legal rights. Women tend to bear the brunt of poverty and discrimination, and Oxfam funds many women's groups working to defend their rights. All Oxfam projects are assessed for their impact on women.

Oxfam Trading is responsible for supplying the crafts and foods sold in Oxfam shops and through the mail order catalogue.

In the UK and Ireland Oxfam raises money for its work from donations, from sales of goods donated to Oxfam shops and from fundraising events and activities. Oxfam works also to raise awareness about the causes of poverty through its education and campaigining work.

OXFAM AND FAIR TRADE

In its work overseas, Oxfam is constantly reminded of how the odds are stacked against poor people. Everywhere they turn, there are barriers which stop them breaking out of poverty, so Oxfam is working to remove the barriers. Some of the hardest to overcome are those which relate to international trade.

The economies of almost all the countries where Oxfam works in the South are dependent on primary commodities such as sugar, coffee and tin. If prices of such commodities on the world market are low, then it's not surprising that the countries that depend on them (and the families that produce them), are poor. When prices we pay in the shops go down, it's a welcome relief, but it's almost always at the expense of the poor.

The people working in these industries are generally powerless. They have no control over the world market that so affects their lives. Oxfam is campaigning and lobbying in the UK and Ireland to secure changes in the rules of international trade – most notably in recent years, to help protect the interests of Windward Island producers in the renegotiation of the European Community's banana-trading rules.

Oxfam is giving practical help to producers in the South. One of the ways of supporting them is through trade – *fair trade.*

Fair trade is about giving people power. It's about fair trade for the people who make or grow a product: the woman who spends all day sewing up shirts, or the family which carefully tends a few coffee plants. They are at the far end of a long line of middlemen and international trade agencies – out of sight and out of mind.

For 30 years, Oxfam Trading has had a special programme of support for just such producers. It is known as Bridge.

Bridge works with producers in Asia, Africa, Latin America, and the Caribbean: providing an export outlet for their crafts and foods; and helping to improve their access to the local market. To make its trade fair, Oxfam Trading:

- buys directly from the producers
- helps them to assess all their costs and reach an acceptable price for their product
- pays an advance on the value of their goods so they can buy raw materials and pay wages without getting into debt
- gives grants so that groups can develop and expand, and distributes an annual bonus
- provides a programme of support, for instance giving advice and information on design and business management.

OXFAM'S FINANCE

Where The Money Comes From

Oxfam's total income for the year to 30 April 1993 was £78.9 million – a new record.
Donations from supporters accounted for 40 per cent of total income.
Net income from the sale of donated goods through the shops, and from the sale of Christmas cards and imported handcrafts through our Trading subsidiary, accounted for 30 per cent of total income.
The British Government's Overseas Development Administration (ODA) and the European Union (EU) provided £8.536 million and £4.578 million respectively.
Oxfam received donations of warm clothing worth £2.5 million to dispatch to needs families during the Cold Front Appeal in the winter of 1992/93.

Where The Money Goes

About two-thirds of the grants made in 1992/3 were for development projects, and one-third for emergencies. Over the last five years an average 79.5 per cent of total income has been made available for Oxfam's staff and grants to local agencies; and education and campaigning programmes in the UK and Ireland to ensure that our supporters are aware of the causes of poverty and the impact of the North on the development of the Third World. (Five per cent of Oxfam's income is allocated to this latter task.)

OXFAM SHOPS AND HOW THEY WORK

Oxfam shops are best known for selling second-hand clothes and goods, but they do much more. They are a collection point for clothes or donations during Oxfam emergency appeals; they promote fair trade through sales of Oxfam Trading goods; and they sell approximately 15 million Christmas cards every year!

There are 26,000 volunteers helping to run Oxfam's 836 shops. In 1992/3 income from the shops contributed £18.25 million for Oxfam's work overseas.

Oxfam is one of the major recycling networks in the country. Everything that arrives at an Oxfam shop is recycled one way or another. Clothes, books, and bric-à-brac are carefully sorted and sold in the shops. Stamps and coins are collected by the shops and re-processed in the Bicester warehouse, where a group of volunteers sort for valuation. Most of these are then eventually either sold at the shops or through stamp and coin fairs.

Wastesaver is Oxfam's recycling plant based in Huddersfield. Every week, the plant processes 80 tonnes of used clothing, 95 per cent of which comes from the Oxfam shops. Textiles are sorted, baled and sold on to specialist recycling units. Rags can be processed to make stuffing for furniture, wool is shredded, then carded and spun once more into yarn. Wastesaver also plays an important role in preparing container-loads of garments to be sent overseas for use in emergency situations.

Each year, Wastesaver sends about 60 tonnes of *aluminium* bottle tops, foil containers, ring pulls, and cans to be recycled. They are melted down and sold to the steel industry to be used in the smelting process.

HOW YOU CAN HELP

Volunteer in your local Oxfam shop or Regional Office. Volunteering for just a few hours a week is a very valuable contribution to Oxfam's work.

Give goods to your Oxfam shop to be sold – and ***buy*** something too!

Buy gifts from the Oxfam Trading ***Mail order catalogue***. To obtain the latest catalogue, ring 0869 245011.

Send a ***donation***.

Take out a ***covenant***: this four-year promise provides Oxfam with regular income and enables us to claim a tax rebate.

Join the ***Oxfam Campaigns Network***: a network of people concerned about poverty who want to help change things for the better. Oxfam Campaigners have helped to promote fair trade, and have written to MPs and decision makers on issues affecting the poor: poverty and conflict; threats to the environment; government aid; Third World debt. For further details contact:

Oxfam Campaigns Network
274 Banbury Road
OXFORD
OX2 7DZ

Take part in Oxfam ***fundraising events***: help with the annual Oxfam Week collection or the annual Fast; take part in sponsored events; organise your own fundraising activities; run a stall at a summer fete. Your Oxfam Regional Office will be pleased to give you details.

The Oxfam Midlands Regional Office is at:

17–20 Burleigh Street
Cambridge
CB1 1DG
01223 358758